42 TRUE TIPS – TALES – AND GUIDE TO FINDING MORE TREASURE!

By

Phil Goodson Sr.

First Edition

METAL DETECTING!
42 TRUE TIPS -TALES AND GUIDE TO FINDING MORE TREASURE!
BY PHIL GOODSON SR.

The Classic Guide to Finding More Treasure for Both the Novice and the Experienced Detectorists!

Dedicated to my lovely wife Maria and daughter Alexandria for their patience, understanding and undeniable support!

By Phil Goodson Sr.

<u>Sell More and Make More!</u>

<u>Best Cash Business!</u>

Introduction

I wrote this short, easy to read reference book as a quick guide for those who are currently active and for those interested in getting involved in the unusual sport of metal detecting. I have included 42 meaningful True Tips as you read along.

Unlike a typical book that has a content page for reference, I wrote this in a personal story format that would have been the type of conversation we would have had if we were sitting down together over lunch. More personal than the usual read.

The 42 True Tips along the way are referenced as they pertain to the subject matter of True Tales as each story is being discussed.

I tried not to embellish any story and related each one to you as accurately and as concisely as possible. Undoubtedly, you will create your own stories and experiences as you begin your new hobby! Hopefully, you will find this book both interesting and informative!

Good luck in your quest of finding treasure! Remember what your parents always mentioned on your family trips....it's all about the journey!

God Speed!

Phil Goodson Sr.

2016

How it All Began

We had just returned from my dad's funeral and this was the first time in ten years that I had even spoken to my brother Fred. We had been estranged for ridiculous reasons but my dad's death seemed to be the moment of reconciliation. Two hard heads finally realizing we're not going to live forever, so we might as well bury the hatchet, so to speak, and get on with life. As I sat there at his kitchen table, it felt strange to be in a home that I knew I should be in, but hadn't visited in a very long time. So many things had passed during that tumultuous ten year period. I wondered how I would begin picking up that slack of time and start the relationship all over again. As he was getting me a cup of coffee, I began looking around and seeing pictures and items that caught my attention. One wooden frame on the wall had a glass cover and behind that glass were about 30 different religious metals and various other metal artifacts about the same size. Crosses, earrings, and other metal items that obviously belonged to someone else, but here they were, inside that case hanging on the wall. Interesting, I thought as I waited for my coffee. (Strange how coffee or tea seems to be the universal connection for almost any occasion but, for this one, it served as an even more important bridge for two brothers who hadn't said a civil word to each other for ten long years!)

Fred actually began the conversation as any host should do just about the same time that he noticed me looking at the wooden frame on the wall with all those different metals inside. He said, "Know where I got those?" I said, "No idea." He told me he had found them metal detecting in the water at a local beach area. A beach that I had visited hundreds of time as I was growing up. I was curious when he first said that he was metal detecting, and secondly, in the WATER! So I replied, "How in the world did you do that and how long did it take you?" And so, after ten long years, our relationship resumed around the topic of metal detecting.

Strange how life's situations cause relationships of both friend and family to turn sour at times and remain that way until some event causes them to reconnect. Never in a million years would I have thought that I would have spoken to my brother again. But, as fate would have it, here I was in his kitchen, sharing a cup of coffee and both of us trying to fill the ten year gap of our lives. Forgiveness has a healing power not only for the one who was forgave, but also for the one doing the forgiving! Not an easy task but great rewards if accomplished.

As I write this book, Fred is in the hospital with chronic illness, pain and discomfort. I can only hope that his health somehow gets better and he is able to have a many more years left to enjoy his family and friends.

Times like these make us aware of all the precious moments that are wasted on such ridiculous and negative feelings of all involved. Moments that we will never ever get back! There are no do-overs in life and the clock of time continues to move forward with or without each of us!

Unfortunately, we have to live a long time to gain the wisdom to work through difficult times and to fully understand how and why we argue with each other, but nonetheless, here I was, discussing the strange hobby of metal detecting with him.

The more he described his hobby, the more I became interested and amazed of his results and I couldn't wait to hear more! I thought to myself, how could I duplicate what

Fred had been doing and find my own treasure? Is it really possible?

Fred handed me something that resembled a fanny pack and I asked him what that was for? "It's for all the treasure you'll find' he said. I was thinking, yeah, right. He expects me to find THAT much stuff that I will actually need a pack to carry it in? I thought to myself, ok...I'll see since it sounds so interesting. Attached to the fanny pack was a garden scoop. Apparently, this was the tool that I was going to use to dig out the treasure once I located it. It had its own holster alongside the pack. Then he handed me the actual metal detector itself. It looked like something out of a science class project with a bunch of buttons and dials and a huge coil on the bottom. In fact, he had several metal detectors capable of land and water searches. "Where are we headed?" I asked. He said the local ball field. So, I gathered up everything he gave me and headed out the door.

We went to a ball field in a local town with the name of Clay. The reason the town had that name is because the soil is heavy packed clay. I soon learned just how hard the packed soil was. As I got out of the car, I turned the detector on and leaned it against the side of the car so that I could put my fanny pack on and, as I did, the darn thing started to make a beeping sound. I thought, ok, the metal from the car itself is causing it to beep. So I moved it away and, as I did, I looked down at the coil and there was a dime! Much to my surprise, the detector had located a dime exactly where I set it down as I was getting set up. I thought to myself, what a fluke. Uncanny actually! My first actual find and it was a coin that I would never have seen since it was the exact color of the gravel I stood upon. Strange how coins sometimes camouflage themselves as they lay upon the ground over time. One can walk over them hundreds of times and never see anything that resembles a coin.

I learned my very first lesson at that moment and here's **Tip #1:**

While searching specifically for money, look for shapes out of character, and not for the actual coins themselves. A round object laying among straight edged shaped gravel is much easier to see, even though it's the exact same color as everything around it. The same rule holds when you dig an object in the dirt. When searching through the handful of dirt, feel for the coin that is round as you wouldn't be able to actually see it unless it's gold or bright silver. I know this sounds crazy and basic, but believe me, trying to locate a coin you've dug up can be a very frustrating experience, especially when you know the coin is right there in front of you and you can't seem to find it. One way to make it even easier is my next tip.

Tip #2: *Spend a little more and get yourself a pin pointer. They can cost anywhere from $50-200, but having one saves a lot of time and effort, cuts down on the amount of digging you have to do, and gives you more free time to actually hunt. I have one attached to my own detector and a hand held one to use with my other detector that doesn't have one attached. Either way, I wouldn't have been able to find as much treasure as quickly as I have without the use of a pin pointer.*

Fred only gave me a quick 5 minute lesson on the correct way to hunt with a detector as he seemed eager to get going himself. I watched him walk to the far end of the ball field, so I decided to go toward a volleyball sand area with the net still up that was surrounded by freshly mowed grass. As I approached the sand pit, the detector went off again. This was my second hit thus far and I couldn't see what the heck was causing it to go off. There was just grass under the coil.

But I remembered what Fred had told me.

Tip #3 *Detectors never lie. They'll locate a metal object and it's up to you to find out what exactly what that object is.* Simple as that! As the beeping in my ear phones continued, I knew that some type of metal was under there. I just had to dig it up and see what it was.

As I crisscrossed the target, the beeping narrowed to the center of the coil and I made a mental note of the spot on the ground in my mind as I moved the coil to the side and laid it down. His pointer showed me I was right on target, so I took his garden spade and cut a nice, small, round plug area and lifted the entire clump of clay from the ground.

Tip #4 *Save your money and buy a pointer! It's a valuable tool worth every penny and it will save you time, effort, and money. Also, it cuts down on the damage you make to the target area while cutting a plug around your target. When searching with a 10" coil on your detector, the pin pointer narrows the search area to an inch or so and you can locate your target in no time! No need to dig some big hole to locate a small coin or piece of jewelry.*

As I started to pull it apart, I noticed a small strip of yellow metal about 1/4 inch wide embedded in the clay. Without any hesitation, I put the clump of dirt in my pocket and scurried over to my brother to ask him what he had found so far. He said he had found an Indian Head and three memorial pennies and asked me what I had found. I took out the clump of dirt and handed it to him and asked what he thought. "Are you kidding me?" he said, "That's gold! You've found your first gold ring!" Then we broke the dirt away as slowly as we could trying to

8

savor the moment and enjoy the rush we were feeling as the ring came out in full view.

What a feeling! Turns out, it was an 18K gold wedding band with no identification! Imagine that? My first time out with a detector that I didn't even own and the very first treasure I found while actually hunting with a detector (the dime I found earlier while leaning the detector against the car didn't count as a hunted object...and I thought *THAT* was a nice find, Ha!) turned out to be GOLD! It was at that moment Fred turned and said to me "You're hooked! There's no turning back now!" How right he was, for this was just the beginning!

From that moment forward, all I could think about was how much time could I devote to both land and water searches for treasure? What kind of detector should I start with? How much did I want to spend or, better yet, could I really afford a decent detector so I could continue this new found hobby? Where would I start hunting? What about the water searches? I had no idea how involved the sport of metal detecting could be. I had so many questions without answers that I felt a little overwhelmed as to where to actually begin, but I also knew I would research and find out all those answers. And so, for me, the hobby of metal detecting was born in my mind and to this day, it has never gotten old, tired or unenjoyable. That is the reason for this book. If you are reading this then chances are you are where I was back then. You have a mind full of questions and nowhere to really begin without sounding like a nimrod asking a bunch of foolish questions to those strange people who walk around beaches with black socks, sandals and a metal detector! Ha!

The first thing I needed to know was....how does a metal detector actually work. Without going into specific detail, the cliff note version is this: The coil emits a signal straight into the ground and when that signal is interrupted by a metal object, it breaks the signal and the result is a beep or tone, depending on the make and model of the machine. The more expensive the machine, the more signals, hence the more finds and the deeper the penetration.

Tip #5: *Find out everything and anything you ever wanted to know about metal detecting on YOUTUBE or metal detecting forums. There's a ton of information and terrific videos of treasure hunters showing you how, where, and when to find buried treasure. I'm just not sure what is actually true and not staged. You'll have to judge that for yourself.*

There is one thing you can count on with this book. Everything I tell you is the truth. I don't lie and I don't steal. That's a fact.

Once you've become comfortable with some knowledge about metal detecting, you can then go shopping for your first one. Always plan on upgrading later. Like any activity that requires the proper equipment, metal detecting is no different and it won't be long before you'll have the itch to get the latest and greatest machine on the market.

Make a personal goal of how much you must find before you start to think about upgrading and spending money. Get to know your detector inside and out. Get to the point where you can tell the difference in the ring tones. I've seen many detectorists who find a lot of jewelry and coins with inexpensive detectors. They rely on their instincts and patience. Patience pays off! The slower and closer you swing your coil the ground the more treasure you'll find. Simple as that. I had an older detectorist tell me, "Go as slow as you can, and then go slower!" Trust me, it's a lot harder to do than you think!

It becomes extremely hard to do when you are in an area where, other detectorists are currently hunting! You'll occasionally look up to see if they're digging for treasure and when you get the chance, you'll try and get close enough to ask them how they're doing. Usually, detectorists are very friendly and welcome the conversation when time allows.

I was working the hard pan area of a beach in Maine one morning and I noticed a young guy hardly ever stopping to dig a target. I was finding an unusual amount of coin, so I yelled up to the guy to come down and search by me since I was having a lot of enjoyment and finding lots of coins. He was so glad I did, for it wasn't long after he arrived that he too was digging targets just like myself.

There's plenty of treasure in the ground for everybody and no one detectorist can find it all. Besides, metal detecting is so much more than just trying to find as much money as you can. Friendship is priceless!

I bought my first detector off the Internet. It was capable of being used on both land and in the water. I paid about $650 for it and was extremely anxious to get it delivered and to start using it. I figured I would buy the best I could afford at the time, therefore saving me a lot of valuable time and to be able to locate targets quicker. You can buy detectors from $50 up but for the rule of thumb with anything in life that you really want to spend a lot of your precious time doing, try the next tip:

Tip #6: *Buy the best you can afford and usually, you won't be disappointed.*

Tremendous values are now offered on the Internet and through craigslist and eBay. However, be careful and do your research first. There's no sense in buying an expensive machine because of the name brand only find out that you have no desire to learn how to actually use it because it's so complicated! I've seen this scenario many times.

Everyone's tolerance and learning level is different. It all depends on how much you really enjoy detecting. Most people think that an expensive machine will automatically locate tons of treasure. Well, if the truth be known, the machines will definitely locate metal, it's just a question of what metals and how deep do you have to dig to find them. Remember, even the least expensive machines don't lie. They just don't tell you what they've located. That's up to you to find out. That learning curve will separate the amateurs from the serious, and usually in a very short time span. The result? After a few hunts, the machine ends up in the closet or on the Internet for sale. Too bad, but then again, I always said that if metal detecting was easy and carefree and finding treasure was abundant, everybody and his brother would be doing it. It's not for the faint of heart or the person who is self-conscious. It takes a certain individual who can withstand all the elements associated with metal detecting to really enjoy the sport. That's not to say that the occasional hunter can't have a good time, but everyone is different.

I have had many conversations with people who would really like to try metal detecting but were uneasy at walking around with a stick in their hand and everyone watching them.

I'm aware of the typical visual stereotype that comes to most peoples' minds when it comes to metal detecting. It's usually some old heavy set guy with black socks and sandals walking among the sunbathers on the beach picking up pocket change.

Well, times have changed and yes, there may still be those that fit that profile, however, with all of the sophisticated machines on the market today, metal detecting has taken on a whole new dimension!

Most detectors today are actually mini computers that can read the ground soil depth and tell you exactly how deep the target is and possibly show you what that target might be. The settings on the sophisticated detectors are sometimes difficult for us older folks to navigate at first, but for the young people of today, it's just another high tech machine!

Give yourself some time and do proper research. Enjoy your journey of finding your first metal detector. You won't be disappointed with your selection and if there's one thing you'll have to conquer, that is patience! You'll need plenty of patience if metal detecting becomes your new activity.

Patience did not and still does not come easy for a type "A" personality like me, but I've learned there's so much more to this great sport! You will too!

What is Considered Treasure?

The word treasure conjures up different things for all people. Some may think of a gold bar or a pirate's booty. Others may think of coins or jewelry or relics of yesteryear. Still, some may be content with calling treasure anything they find, for the "unknown" is what drives a lot of detectorists to continue the sport. I myself, find that whatever target I discover is a treasure unto itself. Whether it's trash like a pull tab, foil, bottle caps, soda cans, nails, or simply an old piece of tin just to name a few of the thousands of trash items you will find, hearing a beep and wondering what the actual target may be is enough for me to stay active in this crazy hobby!

Tip # 7: *Some machines claim they can identify the target before you dig, however, be careful. Depending solely on what the machine says could cause you to miss some very important targets. For instance, pull tabs of aluminum have a similar ring tone as gold. Can you imagine passing over a strong signal when your machine indicates that it's a piece of foil when in fact it's a gold or silver ring? Learn your machine's ring tones and what they identify but do be sure.....take the time and dig everything!*

I have a good friend who bought a new machine and was very anxious to go detecting, so he called me and asked where he should start hunting. I told him I'd pick him up and take him to several local spots. He couldn't wait to begin finding targets like the ones I showed him from my collection. The first place I took him was a local flea market area that had tall grass everywhere and a bunch of debris all over the pace. It didn't look very inviting, but he eagerly trusted my judgement and we began to hunt. After about an hour of finding pull tabs, bottle caps, foil paper and one memorial penny, he began to get discouraged, so he came over to me to see what I had found. I showed him about $1.80 in clad coins (*clad coins are coins that are minted with a copper core and an outer layer that is made of copper and nickel*) along with a few trash items. He quickly saw the contentment on my face and wondered why he was only able to find trash and no coin or jewelry. I explained to him that he's got to know his machine inside and out and what each ring tone means. It should have been the first thing he did before he headed out for his first hunt.

Tip # 8: *When you get your new machine, it's always good to lay out several different coins and trash on the ground where you know there are no targets under the soil and learn the different ring tones as you pass over each target. Becoming familiar with each different signal will help you in the field as you dig each target and discover that your hunch was right. You can also lay your machine on a chair and do the same test as you wave each target by the coil. Just be sure you're not wearing any jewelry on your hand as you do the air test.*

I decided to take him to a different area. An area I had passed many times but hadn't had the chance to visit until this day. It was a field used for soccer, baseball and a handball court included. I knew that there was a lot of activity there so we should have better luck. (Luck to me means Labor-Under-Correct-Knowledge) I told him to envision what the area would have looked like hundreds of years ago. The big oak trees were probably saplings and chances are, the area looked completely different. Also, consider where the children would have been playing. Where would the adults have gathered and be sure to check those areas first. He agreed and we both began to hunt. Conditions were ideal. Sunny day, warm breeze, no one around, and all the grassy area we wanted was waiting for our machines to locate some lost treasure. And so the hunt began. Every once in a while, I would glance over to see how my friend Jim was doing and he seemed to be actively digging away. I watched him stuff a few items in his pouch, so I figured he was finally on his way to learning the art of metal detecting with his new machine.

As I watched Jim, I continued detecting toward a big old oak tree and thought to myself, would anyone have sat or played in and around that tree over all these years? Maybe just getting out of the shade on a sunny day like today would be a relief? The closer I got to that tree I located several quarters. When I'm

15

finding quarters, it tells me several things. First, other detectorists have not been in this area and, if they had, they missed a lot of targets, and second, and here's another tip:

Tip # 9: _Never forget this statement,_ especially, when you feel _discouraged, or see a number of detectorists in the same area, or if you're not finding any targets. You can't find everything! There's always something overlooked. You can hunt and re-hunt the same area over and over again, and although the targets may be fewer, nonetheless, there's targets there waiting to be found. The ground has a funny way of hiding its booty and only the determined detectorist will be able to find the treasure. Do not give up! Keep searching, for I can't tell you the number of times I've watched others hunt all around me and I still end up finding targets in the same area. I'm sure I've missed a lot too. Again, and let me repeat....**You can't find everything!**_

I came across a strong signal about 3 inches in the ground so I started to dig a plug (a plug is a semi-circular cut in the ground _around_ the target so when you lift the plug, chances are the target is either in that plug of dirt or just below. There's less chance of scratching the target when using the plug system of digging and easier to cover your tracks when you leave.)

Tip # 10: _Without exception, always fill in every single hole you dig! Leaving a hole exposed will lead to many more restrictions to areas that others will not be able to hunt and gives metal detecting a bad reputation._

As I raised the plug I noticed the bottom revealed a silver ring band. I said to myself...."Sweeeeet" (a comment I usually make when I've discovered treasure!) Instead of removing all the dirt, I wanted my friend Jim to see what I had found exactly as I had found it so he would also recognize the same when HE finds similar jewelry. Also, to show him that metal detecting targets do not always result in pull tabs, trash or other useless items.

By not taking the ring completely out of the dirt plug, I was able to savor the discovery of that moment. Something I have a tendency to do when finding treasure! Why not? It's fun, harmless, and exciting to wonder what the object will actually look like when fully exposed. I do this same thing in my water hunts which I'll explain in detail later in this book.

Jim took a look at the plug and I could see his interest peak as I removed the dirt from around the ring. It turned out to be a beautiful diamond studded school ring with initials inscribed inside. To be honest, to me, it looked quite ostentatious for a school ring. But, nonetheless, when I discover jewelry that has a name inscribed on it, I always try to locate the owner. Jim then realized that he too could find treasure just like I do, so he immediately got back to his hunt and as the day progressed, Jim found lots of coins and yes, some trash but unfortunately, no rings for Jim this particular day. That discovery would have to wait for another hunt.

As for that school ring, I had my daughter call the owner and tell him that her father had found it. I didn't want to call a high school aged boy myself for any reason. That thought made me uncomfortable. Funny thing is what his response was. He told my daughter he did indeed lose the ring but didn't want it back. Ouch! I can only figure that the ring must have been a gift that he didn't want or it looked too gaudy for his age or worse yet, conjured up bad memories. Bottom line is that I kept the ring and added it to my collection. A nice addition to the hundreds of others!

My Box of Tears

Looking at all of the jewelry that I have found, I gave my collection the above name, for I can only imagine what the owners of all the jewelry felt like the moment they realized they had lost their jewelry. Sadness, disappointment, frustration, self-blame for possible carelessness that caused them to lose it in the first place? Not really sure, but either way, I always think of what happened at that very moment that their coins or jewelry became lost. I know how I feel when that happens and I have to admit, it's an uneasy and sometimes sickening feeling. I had put my favorite Tommy Bahama waterproof watch on top of my car as I was taking off my wet suit after a shallow water hunt and then I drove off with the watch still on top of the car. Never to be found again. Augh! Boy, do I miss that watch. I loved it and hoped that one day I would find it again, but no luck so far. So, I've rationalized like all the others who have lost something they really loved. I realize that someone else may be enjoying my misfortune or maybe it hasn't been found by anyone yet and is just simply gone! Who knows? Maybe one day I'll find it myself.

I can recall just about every emotion I felt when finding each coin or piece of jewelry. It's amazing how deep the feeling is when you really enjoy something to the point that you can remember even the smallest detail of that experience. I have thousands of clad coins and interesting items I've yet to research. Then it dawns on me that every single item was located and recovered one piece at time. That's a lot of digging! I'm talking thousands of items! Treasure usually doesn't come in groups unless you find a coin spill, but even they're rare and you'll really appreciate one when you do. Put the time in and enjoy your sport of metal detecting. You'll be rewarded many times over in many different ways. It's not always about the money. A great experience is priceless. One day you'll have your own box of tears!

A Guy Named Randy

While shallow water hunting at a local marina, a gentleman came up to me and asked me, "Hey, how deep does that thing go?" I replied "It goes 300 feet deep but I don't. Why do you ask?" He said that his friend had just lost his new 15th anniversary wedding band at the sand bar where the volleyball net was located and wanted to know if I could help him find it. Of course, I said yes but I didn't have a boat. He suggested that he and his friend take me out to the sand bar in their boat. So, I waited about 30 minutes for his friend (Randy) to arrive with the boat. Once he got there, I climbed into the boat with two complete strangers and they took me to a spot I didn't even know existed on a local lake.

As we crossed the lake it seemed like a long time and pretty far out so I was thinking that if these two guys tried anything, I'd have to throw them both overboard and take their boat back to shore. I know it sounds strange, but when you live your life teaching martial arts and have a 3rd degree Black Belt, you live a life of always being aware of current situations and everything around you at all times. It's sort of living in a "locked and loaded" frame of mind and, believe me, it may be good to be confident but it's really embarrassing when you suddenly react to an innocent gesture, such as an unexpected shoulder tap or hand shake. I find myself apologizing immediately after those close encounters and explain why they take place. Most people are understanding while others just think I'm nuts. The flip side is that I can go anywhere, do anything and feel confident that I can handle the situation. It's reassuring to know how to handle situations if needed and I can hunt places most people wouldn't venture into like me, especially alone. Studying martial arts as a life style has its rewards and I wouldn't have it any differently!

"Enough about me talking about me....so, what do YOU think of me?' Ha! That's a crazy line I always use and it usually brings some chuckles. I have a sick sense of humor but it also has its just rewards.

As it turned out, the two guys I was with were very nice and I quickly realized that they only sought my help in a tough situation. As we approached the sand bar I could see hundreds of boaters and swimmers in the shallow water. Most were popping beer cans and drinking with floating cocktail tables holding their drinks, and eating finger food. This was some sand bar! Not being a boater, I guess I didn't understand the mentality of the boater's lifestyle, but soon came to know how they have a unique way of congregating among themselves and having a great time on the water that most people can't get reach, and only accessible by boat.

I thought to myself, there must be a zillion bottle caps and pull tabs on the bottom of this swim area since this is the local hot spot. (BTW....pull tabs were invented in 1939 and they are one of the biggest nuisances to a metal detectorist! They are everywhere! Worse yet, they have the same ring tone as GOLD, so if you think you can just ignore them, you can, but you'll miss finding gold rings and jewelry). I dig everything).

I hopped off the boat into the water which was about three feet deep. No problem, but as I started detecting toward the volleyball net area, everyone looked at me as if I was an alien who just came from Mars with this long handled contraption of a scoop and multi colored long handled stick with a big round thing on the end. It has lots of different knobs near the top. Not to mention the two big cups covering my ears. The only thing I had in common with everyone around me was the baseball cap and sunglasses that I was wearing. If you're the type of person who doesn't like people staring at you and asking you questions, then you might consider finding another hobby. Most people have no problem walking up to you while you're detecting and asking..."Hey, whatta ya finding? Anything good?"....or "What's that thing?"....or "Excuse me, what do you expect to find?"

Tip # 11: *Regardless of what you find or how valuable you may think it is, or how proud you are of finding it......don't ever tell a stranger what you've actually found, or begin describing it to them in detail! Simple as that! You'll pay a heavy price for answering their questions. They may claim your discovery as the one they lost, or they know the person who lost it, or they'll be jealous that you're finding jewelry in an area that they are in at the moment. The reasons for not telling strangers are endless but use common sense when replying to their inquisitive minds. The best answer is (and remember, I don't lie) I'm finding some pocket change, pull tabs and bottle caps. That's usually the truth anyway! I just don't mention that I've found anything valuable for it causes concern to those around you. No need to bring any more attention to yourself than you already have by just being there! One line I usually say to people who try and follow me or watch me closely is..."Hey, stay in school and get a good education and you won't have to do this for a living!" That usually brings a smile to everyone's face, young and old!*

The closer I got to the volleyball net, the more trash I found. As always, I remove the trash and put it in my pouch to bring back to shore and then throw it away. I also started finding small coins and even a pair, yes, a pair, not one, of silver earrings. The more I searched around the volleyball net, the more loose change I began finding. That told me that chances were, not many detectorists had been in this area and the targets were plentiful. I continued to search for about two hours and kept finding lots of coin and trash combined, but no gold wedding band that belonged to Randy. We headed back to shore and Randy couldn't thank me enough for my time and effort and as we got off the boat and walked ashore, Randy took out a one hundred dollar bill and started to hand it to me.

I politely refused the cash and suggested that he pay it forward and only under the condition that whoever he was paying it forward to would NOT know that it was HIM who was the one doing the kind act. Randy seemed a little puzzled but I explained to him, that doing something for someone without seeking credit has its own rewards and one can never appreciate that feeling unless they have done it themselves.

Randy said he would do that and as we parted, I asked him for a business card. I told him that if I ever found his 15th anniversary gold wedding band, regardless of how much time had passed, I gave him my word that I would return it to him. He seemed like he wanted to believe me, but cautiously agreed as we shook hands and both parted.

About three weeks later, a friend of mine, Paul, was taking his boat out of the water for the season on that same lake and asked me if I would like to go for a ride. I said sure, so we met about 6 AM. I asked him, just for giggles, could he take me over to that sand bar where all the boaters gather. I explained the story of Randy and his gold wedding band. Paul said absolutely no problem and that he would take me there. Paul brought a book to read while I was searching around the volleyball net, only this time there were no other boaters or swimmers in the water which made it much easier for me to wade around. I tried to imagine where Randy's ring would have ended up if he had just served the ball as he originally told me. I looked in areas that seemed too far away for a ring to be thrown. Once on the other side of the net and about 20 feet away, I hit a target that had a loud signal of gold. Thinking to myself, as I dug under the water, that it's probably another pull tab like the ones I had been finding a few weeks back.

The water was extremely calm and it was a beautiful sunny morning. As I raised my scoop up out of the water, I expected to find another pull tab. I watched as the sand and mud sifted out the sides of my water scoop as I usually do and, as the dirt disappeared, I began to see the bottom with no target visible. However, there in the very corner of the scoop was a beautiful, shiny gold object the shape of a ring. At this point, my heart began pumping a little harder than usual. The same way it does every time I see any jewelry in the bottom of my scoop. It's a great feeling! Sort of like finding a pearl in an oyster! What a moment. Wanting to savor that special time as I always do, I didn't actually take the ring out of the scoop but took the scoop over to the boat where Paul was reading his book and showed him the scoop with the ring still in the bottom corner among the silt.

Paul's jaw dropped! I told him this is why I do this sport! Regardless of how much trash and how many useless targets I find, finding one ring wipes out all the memories of the trash found and reignites my enthusiasm to continue searching. Sort of like the game of golf. Have a miserable first 17 holes and then pull off a birdie on the eighteenth and you're golden! You leave the course happier than a clam at high tide!

When I looked at the ring more closely, I thought to myself that this couldn't possibly be Randy's ring for he said his ring was just a simple gold band. I pictured a typical gold wedding band similar to the ones I usually find, plain, gold, with no markings. Well, this ring was your basic yellow gold alright, but it also had white gold on each side and also had diamonds! Based on Randy's original description, there was no way that this particular ring could be Randy's ring!

As Paul and I headed back to the shoreline, I thought to myself, how lucky I was be searching for one ring and end up finding another one that's even more valuable than the one I was originally looking for. I started to think of what the ring was worth and how my wife had been suggesting that we need new family room furniture. I usually don't sell my jewelry but this time was different.

As soon as I got home, just for giggles and to reassure my own mind that his was not Randy's ring, I got Randy's card and gave him a call. I told Randy I had found a gold wedding band in the sand bar area but it probably wasn't his and asked him to describe in more detail exactly what his anniversary ring looked like.

"Well Phil, it's more than just a gold band and I should have given you a better description when I first told you. It has yellow gold as the band and white gold on the sides with several diamonds embedded on each side. "I said, "Bummer" and he asked me, "Why?" I replied...."Because that's the exact description of the ring I now have on my finger!" He said "you've gotta be $#@#$% me, really?" I said, "Yup."

We decided to meet at the same marina that night at 9:00 o'clock so I cleaned up the ring with some special jewelry cleaner and it looked absolutely beautiful! I had a nice ring box and put it inside looking like the day they first bought it, and I headed to the marina that night.

When we met, Randy's wife was there too and I said to both of them, "Well, I'm so glad I found this for you and, as I give this back to you, there's one condition." He says, "What's that?" I said with a smile, "If I ever find this ring again in the water, I'll keep it for myself. Make sure you get it fitted properly or don't wear it in the water again!" We all laughed and agreed. Then Randy handed me an envelope. Inside was a restaurant gift certificate for $100. I decided to accept that and thanked him profusely.

Randy called me several weeks later and told me he had repeated this event to hundreds of people, of how a guy named Phil met a guy named Randy who paid it forward without expecting credit, and how Phil then found his ring! No doubt, Karma working at its finest. Good things happen to good people helping others. The world could use a lot more good Karma in these troubled times!

A Boy, His Dad and a Starfish

As a dad and his son were walking along a sandy ocean beach one morning at sunrise, they noticed hundreds of starfish stranded on the beach. Apparently, high tide had receded too quickly and left hundreds of starfish stranded.

The boy was in a hurry as most five year olds usually are and wanted to run along the beach but the dad stopped and picked up one starfish, looked at it and tossed it out into the ocean. The son said "What are you doing daddy?" The dad replied, "I'm saving this starfish." The little boy then said, "What difference will it make, they're millions of them!" The dad then called the boy over closer and knelt down and said straight into his face with a soft yet firm voice, "I know there's a lot of them, but it made a difference that one." Even at five years old, the little boy understood that even though there were many stranded starfish, his dad could save at least one and that would make a difference to that particular starfish.

The lesson here is that while you're metal detecting, you will find many people who are curious about what you are doing and will ask you lots of questions. Expect it and answer those questions with a smile and with courtesy. Don't be annoyed that someone is bothering you, especially if they are children. You never know how inspirational you can be to a complete stranger and be the very one who makes that person so interested in this unusual activity that they'll go home and buy themselves a detector! Not everyone dislikes detectorists. Most people understand the sport and react to who they currently see, perhaps based on their past encounter with a former detectorist they came in contact with. Keep the good Karma moving forward for all of us in involved with this sport by being courteous and understanding to all around you while searching. You'll have a much more enjoyable experience!

A Wad of Money and Two Kids

I was searching on a Maine beach area with my friend Bob when I noticed two young kids that I figured to be about seven or eight year olds heading toward us. They were about a hundred yards away and I could see by the way they were walking that they were headed straight to us to check us out. As they got closer, I said to Bob "Watch this" as I reached in my pocket and took out my gold money clip that held all my credit cards and cash. It always looks like it's full of cash since you can't see the credit cards because the money is wrapped around them. I took my foot and made a swipe in the sand and dropped my clip and cash in the hole and covered it with sand. As the boys got closer, I could hear them talking and saying, "Wow, wonder what they're finding?" When they finally reached us, they asked the usual question…"Hey, what are you guys finding?" Without answering their question, I just said very quickly, "Stand back, I've got a strong target!" They could hear the beeping of my detector and they quickly tried to maneuver out of the way but yet stay close enough to see what was going on and what all the fuss was about.

They kept peeking around the side of us as the beeping narrowed down to an area that had the treasure beneath! I slowly dug around the sand with my hand and the money clip loaded with credit cards and cash appeared. I took it out of the sand and blew off the sand as the boys watched. Their eyes were as big as saucers and, without hesitation they said, "Holy cow, we're going to tell our dads to get US one of those!" They turned and ran as fast as they could back to wherever they were staying. I can only imagine the conversation they had when they arrived back at their home away from home. Talk about leaving an impression! What a bunch of laughs Bob and I had over that episode! Like many, I'll never forget that moment!

Barry and the Gold Ring

I always carry my metal detector with me when I travel. It's always ready to be turned on and ready go at a moment's notice. Opportunity has a way of appearing unexpectedly and you need to take advantage of every situation.

While traveling with my business partner Barry in Upstate NY near the Canadian border, we were discussing areas to treasure hunt since he was from that area. He mentioned the locks on the St. Lawrence Seaway and how it had a local beach area that he used to go to when he was kid. We happened to be in that same area as we were working, so we drove up into the park area just to take a look for future reference.

I'm not sure what made me do it, but we were looking out over the beach area from the car, and as if the water was calling to me, I decided, just for giggles, to walk to the water's edge with my detector and see what I could find. It was a cold November day and Barry decided to wait in the car. So, with my three piece suit and new wingtips, I took the detector out of the trunk and gingerly walked down to the water's edge so as not to get any mud on my shoes. I put the detector in the water that was about 2 inches deep and 6 inches off the edge of the shoreline. Why there in that exact spot I'll never know but then it happened. I got a heavy gold signal and couldn't believe what I was hearing.

I dug the target with my spade and took out a wad of mud. Since the target was in that wad of mud, I brought it back to the car to show Barry and put my detector back in the trunk. When I opened the plug of mud, there was a gold ring with a sapphire stone on the top and two diamonds on each side nestled deep inside. I'm still not sure why I felt so compelled to stop working and, in my business clothes, take a walk to a beach that I had never been to before, leaving my business partner waiting in my car, and locate a treasure all within a 30 minute time period! Go figure! Truly amazing, and all along Barry thought I was nuts. Who could blame him? Good Karma!

Jimmy and the Silver Spoon

My friend Jimmy suffered a brain injury at birth which has resulted in great physical challenges throughout his life. As a result of his condition he has balance issues and difficulty walking. He really is amazing despite his challenges. He's always off kilter but he's lucky to be walking at all. To be sure he keeps his strength and doesn't feel dependent I never help him up when he falls, for he has too much pride and gets back up on his own. This builds his self-confidence. Jimmy is 30 years old and a great person and true friend!

While detecting on a Maine beach one afternoon, Jimmy was hanging onto my arm as I swung my detector with the other one. We covered the hard pan area (the area between low and high tide) and he brought me good luck. I found two nice gold rings along the way and Jimmy watched and tried to help me dig each target. That was a difficult task for him so I told him I would do it as he watched.

He seemed excited but not as much as I would have thought he would be, until I found a large silver spoon. I handed it to Jimmy and said this is the start of your treasure collection. The rings made no impact, but that spoon seemed to excite him more than anything else. To this day, he recalls that moment on the beach walking arm and arm with me metal detecting together.

At one point he fell backwards into the shallow surf, and as he tried to get up, a young lady ran over and helped him. Wiping the wet sand off of him she said to me, "Didn't you see him fall?" I replied, "Of course I did, but he doesn't need my help getting up." At that time I realized Jimmy was a "chick magnet" and that every girl wants to help him as he struggles to walk a straight line. I always kid Jimmy about his balance and he kids me back about my bad jokes. Jimmy and I have a ton of laughs together and his innocence is so endearing. I enjoy metal detecting with Jimmy.

NY State Troopers Evict Me

I live near a local lake that has a beach guarded by an over protective owner. This makes access for shallow water searching almost impossible or nonexistent. However, having permission to enter the water from the adjacent area allowed me to wander over to the beach swim area via the lake and not cross over the owner's land.

As I approached the swim area I was in shallow water about 60 yards out from the beach and finally located a strong signal. I started to dig and could sense movement back on the shoreline, so I quickly glanced over. I saw the owner jumping up and down on the dock waving his fists in the air yelling something that obviously wasn't pleasant. I removed one ear cup of my headphones and asked him what he had said. He yelled back, "Get the &%#!#@ off my land!" I replied, "You don't own the water!" Well, that didn't sit well with him and the next thing I knew, I heard someone yelling with a megaphone for me to come out of the water! They were two New York State Troopers.

I waded up to the shore and explained to the troopers that I didn't cross his land but, in fact, had permission to enter the water from a nearby homeowner. Also, the fact that the owner doesn't actually own the water. They agreed and said it had been a long day and asked me if I would just move further down the lake to save them from writing a report. I said as a businessman and out of respect for you I will do just that. So I waded to the left about 100 yards and began to search once more.

As luck would have it, my very first target turned out to be a beautiful solid silver wedding band! Imagine that! I was thrown out of one area only to find a nice ring in my new area. Ha! Chances are, I would never have found that ring had it not been for a grumpy old land owner having me change my direction of searching. See, good things sometimes come from negative situations. Never give up!

Nine Detectorists and a School Ring

I arrived late one morning at a local lake after looking forward to being there exactly at the same time the lifeguards would be taking down the rope around the swim area. However, I felt an immediate sense of disappointment as I reached the water's edge. I counted nine other metal detectorists already in the very area I was hoping to search by myself!

Imagine the feeling of waiting all summer long to get permission to search somewhere and then see nine treasure seekers just like me already in the water. Augh! However, I persevered and decided to wade into the water anyway. As I waded through the group, each of whom were about 10 feet from each other, my metal detector was screaming from being too close to everyone's same band frequency, so I continued forward.

As I got closer to them, they started to slowly wade away and give me some room for I'm sure their machines were doing the same thing. Just as I reached the center of the group I unexpectedly hit a strong signal. They saw me hesitate and start to dig. When my scoop reached the surface of the water, I saw the familiar glimmer of gold in the bottom of my scoop!

It was a beautiful 1946 gold school ring with a green emerald stone and a diamond in the center! Wow! Couldn't believe it! Here I was in the middle of all those detectorists and I found this ring! Truly amazing how so many detectorists probably walked right over it and never found it!

Worth repeating here....never give up! Never get discouraged.

Tip #12: *If your coil misses the target by even the slightest margin, the target might as well be on the other side of the earth. There's an old saying among treasure hunters; "If you miss it by an inch, you miss it by a mile!" Hunt slowly and steadily. Be patient!*

Three Gold in the Hardpan

While setting up our beach tents and chairs on our favorite beach in Maine my sister-in-law, Pam, watched me stop to gather my detecting gear and head toward the water. I told her I was going to see what a quick early morning search would bring. Seeing that the tide was way out and that there was a lot of hardpan area exposed, I couldn't miss such an opportunity. I told her I'd be right back.

I hadn't walked twenty feet when I hit a target. When I was done digging, I had found a huge gold college ring about two inches under the hardpan. So excited, I walked back to Pam and showed her. She couldn't believe it. We talked a bit and then I once again began to head out toward the water. I got about 150 feet further than the previous time and I hit another target. That discovery turned out to be a beautiful gold wedding band circled with diamonds! Are you kidding me? How lucky could I be? Either earlier searchers had missed these two gold rings (unlikely) or I was the first one out this particular morning.

Remember, local hunters are on the beaches every single day without exception, so finding two gold rings within 50 yards of each other is extremely rare. I put the ring in chest area of my shorty wet suit.

TIP #13: *Don't put any valuable finds in your usual coin pouch for if anything happens (and eventually it will) losing coins is not as bad as losing jewelry.*

I continued searching only to hit a *third* target that once again turned out to be a gold find! It was a toe ring! Small, but very nice, and it was gold! Three gold finds all in the hardpan, all within 100 yards of our beach area, and all within about an hour! Lady Luck was with me that morning! I returned to Pam and showed her the gold finds and she wouldn't have believe it if she hadn't seen it for herself!

What a great way to start a day at the beach!

Spencer's First Treasure Hunt

I heard the words of my excited six-year-old grandson Spencer, "Hey Grandpa, can you take me metal detecting with you in the morning?" I said, "Of course, but you'll have to get up early." He said, "No problem," and that he would be ready. I've heard that statement before from so many people, but with Spencer, he seemed so serious.

I walked into the kitchen at 6:00 AM and there sat Spencer at the kitchen table. He was all set with his garden spade, pouch and dressed in warm clothes. I took him to a local school that I had seen when arriving the day before. I had never been there before, so we headed toward the playground area and concentrated around the swings and slides. I thought that would be a terrific place to start searching for loose change or jewelry.

Spencer hung by my side for about 20 minutes watching me dig up several coins. I showed him how to do the digging and he dug several himself. He seemed interested at first, but that interest began to wane as we continued away from the playground area. Finally, after about 30 minutes, Spencer looked up at me and said, "Grandpa? I'm bored." Ha! I thought how could he be bored? We're finding coin after coin, but that didn't seem to matter to a six year old. I asked him, "What would you like to do Spencer?" He said, "I'd like to go swinging Grandpa!"

I suddenly realized that his desire to play on the swings was much greater than walking alongside Grandpa. I admired his honesty and said of course, and watched him play as I continued to search the rest of the school yard. Shortly after, we both sat together on a bench and talked about coins, their value and life in general. That moment was a memorable moment for both of us! Metal detecting has a way of finding some things more precious than money or jewelry!

A Father and Son's Diary

I read this story a while back and it touched me deeply, so I'm passing it on to you. I apologize if you've heard it before, but true or not, it's worth the read and the message contained within.

An elderly man had lost his son a while back. He was now in the process of downsizing his own home to purge unwanted items so that he and his wife could relocate to a smaller home. As he was going through his attic and deciding what to keep and what to toss out, he came across his diary from earlier days. He glanced through it and came upon a time that he and his son had stolen the day from work and had gone fishing together. Just the two of them.

He read the words that he had written at the end of that entry: "*Took Rob fishing for the first time and what a terrible day it turned out to be. Rained hard, no fish, tangled lines, but we made the most of it. Got home late, totally soaked, but wished it had been a better day for Rob's first time fishing.*" He remembered how frustrating that day had been with sadness.

A short while later while still in the attic, he came across Rob's diary. Curious and eager to remember his son since he had been gone for many years, he turned to the same date where Rob had written about his first fishing trip with his dad.

It read: "*Had the best time of my life with my dad today. Spent the entire day fishing or should I say trying to fish. Ha! Didn't catch anything but maybe a cold since it rained all day and we ended up getting soaked. Laughed as my dad became more and more upset about the day not being what he had hoped it would be. But to me, it was more about the fact my dad took the day off from work to spend with me. Just me. I will have to say that this day is the best day of my life thus far! Looking forward to many more!"*

The moral here? Enjoy the moments, not the days!

Nephew Zac-Beach-Barber Dime

As he watched me dig countless coins and jewelry, my nine-year-old nephew Zac decided he would like to try metal detecting. Funny how some kids think about what they'd like to do and others just do it. I let Zac use my sand scoop and my first Internet purchased metal detector.

The difficulty with this detector is that all the ring tones are the same. There is no difference between silver, gold or iron so every target has to be dug to be identified. The controls are in the headphones which does give easier arm mobility while detecting. Simple but extremely effective. Find a target and it will metal of some kind. A lot of work for many people, but Zac plowed through it to dig and keep everything the detector located. After a few searches, Zac had accumulated mounds of bottle caps, pull tabs, wires, foil, sinkers, fish hooks, nails, and just about every kind of metal you can imagine! Oh yes, occasionally, he would find some loose change along the way.

His perseverance finally paid off when he found his first REAL ring! On a Maine beach one summer morning, he heard a strong signal and dug into the sand to find a beautiful, silver ring! One that he could be proud of and finally join the ranks as a seasoned treasure hunter! After all, he had paid his dues and, if you could see the tons of non-valuable items he had accumulated thus far, you'd agree!

Zac has since saved up his own money to buy a new, more advanced metal detector and all the accessories. He'll make a deep dent in the vast amount of hidden treasures buried everywhere! He still loves his video games but metal detecting has a special spot in his outdoor activities. Amazing how he shadowed his Uncle Phil metal detecting to the point that he wanted to have his very own detector and find his very own treasures! Truly, a rare occurrence in this fast paced world today!

1830 Old House & George W.

I'm referring to the first George W....Washington! While getting permission to scan this property, which is an old farmhouse built in 1830, I didn't realize just how cold it was until my fingertips became numb inside my latex gloves.

Tip #14: Get yourself a box of hospital quality latex gloves (cost about $8) to wear while searching. You never know what's inside the ground while you're digging and trying to retrieve a target. One can only imagine what's been dumped or deposited in the soil over the years. Gloves give great protection and they are a small investment that pay off well. They can be tossed away after each search. Without them, I've contracted poison ivy and it isn't pretty! You only have to get it once!

I immediately knew that no other detectorist had been in this area because almost every penny I turned up was from the early nineteen hundred era. Old toys and whatnots began to appear as I dug every signal I heard. I dig every signal when searching around old houses since the signals are sometimes confusing. I don't rely on what the detector suggests that the target may be, for in the past, I've found out differently and I've been pleasantly surprised!

One hour and 38 pennies later, I started to wonder how in the world I kept finding all these pennies. Is that all they used to lose at this house or were they just throwing them on the lawn for each wish they made? Nonetheless, finding any coin is a great accomplishment regardless of the denomination.

I finally hit on a target that brought up a strange looking older coin about the size of a quarter. It turned out to be a double-sided George Washington token from 1797! A little rough possibly from a run-in with a lawn mower, but regardless, a nice piece of history! I always think of the last person to have held each coin that I find and wonder how they came to lose it in the first place. Savoring every moment while metal detecting is a huge stress relief for me!

Where Can I Metal Detect?

This is usually the first question I get asked by someone who has just purchased a metal detector. I'll list a few places for you, but with a little imagination, I'm sure you'll start to think of several on your own as you get more involved with your new pastime.

Tip #15: There's no area too small to search. It doesn't matter if it's a small patch of grass alongside the highway or an area only two feet wide in front of a home. There's always the chance that the soil currently there was deposited from another location during construction hundreds of years ago. This is especially true in older homes and properties. Never think that just because you're familiar with the area or that you've lived there all your life that you know for certain the ground holds no treasure. You can be very mistaken. Don't take anything for granted.

Case in point: One Sunday, our local priest told the parish that, the day before, a wedding had been held and the four-year-old ring bearer had somehow lost the bride's gold wedding band. It was lost somewhere between the road and the altar. He asked us to please look around the floor on our way out of the church to see if anyone could locate it. You can imagine what that did to my mind!

I offered my services and was granted permission to search the church grounds. The ring should have been on top of the ground since it had only been lost for one day, however, after carefully searching the small grassy area I didn't find the ring. What I did find was also outstanding! Three Indian head pennies, a rosary ring, which I never knew existed, four clad quarters, two dimes, and a 1797 Connecticut large cent, all in decent condition! All in an area less than twenty feet wide! So, you see, there is no area too small, but there are areas that are too big. In larger areas it's always best to grid a pattern to search rather than just randomly wandering around hoping to find something.

Here are some areas to think about searching:

- Church yards
- Old dump areas
- Beaches
- State Parks (with verbal permission or permits)
- Drive-in-theaters
- Backyards
- Campgrounds
- Flea market grounds
- City sidewalk grass areas
- Farms
- Hunting camps
- Logging trails
- New construction sites
- Old factory grounds
- Old church revival grounds
- State Fair grounds
- Wedding venue grounds
- Shorelines
- Fishing areas
- Under old bridges
- Vacant home property
- Racetrack grounds
- City Parks
- Marinas
- Volleyball court areas
- Baseball fields
- Football fields
- Soccer fields
- School yards
- Friend's & relative's property
- Recent building teardowns
- Forests

Use your imagination and you'll expand on this list considerably. Always ask permission and, as always, fill in all your holes before you leave.

Asking For Permission

Wow, this is one of the most difficult topics to discuss or actually do if you're the least bit shy. If being around people makes you uncomfortable, then your metal detecting experiences may be limited. Oh, you'll always find some treasure, but you'll need to search areas that have not been searched out already by detectorists before you, or to search areas that no one has had access to in a long time, to find some really interesting treasure!

Tip #16: *It's an old cliché but true! "If it was that easy, everyone would be doing it!" Truer words were never spoken. Learn to ask permission and the door of treasure hunting opportunities will open wide for you. Don't let the thought of rejection from a land or home owner stand in the way of your metal detecting experiences!*

Since I've made a lifetime of being involved with sales and marketing, asking permission has always come easy to me. However, hearing the word or phrases "no," or "sorry, I don't think so", or "you won't find anything here" or "not today" or similar turndowns never become routine and always take a little bite out of your personal pride. But that feeling only lasts for about three minutes or until you find that first treasure on the next search! Don't take everything in life so seriously that you can't shake off an occasional turndown now and then.

Remember your first girlfriend or boyfriend? Don't tell me you always got the first kiss easily and without some concerted effort. Looking back I'm sure you'll agree, that at that time, it was well worth all the time and effort you put into it.

Well, metal detecting is your new love now and you'll need to learn how to romance the art of the "asking permission phase" to gain access to new areas that hold hidden treasure!

If you're carrying your detector in your vehicle on a daily basis like I do, then you'll need to hone your skills of stopping and asking a complete stranger if you can search their property. Not an easy task at first, but after a while, you'll become accustomed to hearing an occasional "no". Chances are you'll never see that person again, so big deal if they won't let you search their property.

Walk away proud of the fact you at least you tried and there's always the outside chance that you might be back that way again and have to ask several more times. Be persistent. I've heard a lot more "yes" than "no" and believe me, it's a terrific feeling to know you can search an area that many detectorists passed by simply because they were afraid to ask permission! In my experience, that type of property yields a lot of treasure!

Here are some phrases that I personally use to ask permission to search. I do so with sincerity and not just lip service. (It's funny how someone knows when you really mean what you are saying and not just giving them a line.)

The first thing to remember is that your physical approach sends an important visual signal to the home owner, so try and think of how YOU would feel if someone was asking to walk on YOUR land with a metal detector, dig a hole, and possibly find something of value that belonged to YOU? Imagine how that would feel. Probably pretty strange to say the least!

Tip #17: *"You only have one chance to make a first impression."*

Make it a good one! When approaching the owner, always knock first or ring the doorbell and then, step far enough back (so that you don't intimidate), with your hands clasped in front of you (to show that you have no weapons). This way you look very non-threatening. Then try using some of the following opening lines every time:

"Excuse me Sir. (Miss), Good morning, my name is_____ and I'm kind of a history buff and I was wondering if you'd allow me to scan this area with my metal detector. I know it sounds crazy but I'm looking for old musket balls. I don't make a bunch of holes. In fact, squirrels make more of a mess than me!

"Excuse me Sir. (Miss), good morning. My name is_____ and I'm stealing some time from work for this crazy hobby of metal detecting. I'm a local history buff and was wondering if you'd allow me to scan this area for about 30 minutes? I'm looking for old musket balls and stuff like that.

"Excuse me Sir, (Miss), my name is _____ and I was wondering if I could scan this area with my metal detector? I should be working at the moment but my hobby is much more enjoyable. I'm just looking for old musket balls and such.

Side bar note: One summer day, I was passing a local farmer's land that was adjacent to a historical battle field and I thought to myself, if I was a general with several hundred troops, would this be the best place to camp for the night? Imagine all of the neat stuff in the ground just waiting for a guy like me to come along and find. All of these thoughts were going through my mind and I got so excited I couldn't stand it, so I just had to ask permission to metal detect on this particular property!

I saw the farmer on his tractor, busting his butt, plowing his field, so I started walking right out to the middle of the field to ask his permission. I thought to myself (and your mind will do this too, believe me) he's going to be so aggravated that a complete stranger is walking on his land and bothering him while he's hard at work that he's going to be upset for sure! There's no way this farmer's going to grant me access to his land. Since he's located so close to a historical park, he's probably been pestered countless times by people like me wanting to metal detect on his land. I was so convinced of what he was going to say, that I had my obligatory "Thank you anyway" phrase in my mind all ready to say as I got closer to him.

He had just made a run past me so I had to stand there like a statue in the middle of his field and wait for him to go all the way to the end of his row and return back one row over. It felt like a lifetime. Talk about being embarrassed, augh! It was almost as though he ignored me the first time he went by and purposely made me wait.

Finally, he drove up to me and stopped his tractor. He looked at me with a look on his face that suggested he was thinking "What in the world is this guy doing standing here in the middle of my field?"

I figured it was all or nothing so I had better get it over with quickly, lick my wounds, say thank you anyway and walk back to my car. So I took a deep breath and yelled up to him as he sat on his monster John Deer tractor, about 6ft higher than me, and said, "Excuse me sir, sorry to bother you. Have you ever had a stranger walk up to you in your field and ask you if they could metal detect on your land?" He replied with a simple "Noooo." I said, "Well I am. I'm looking for old musket balls and stuff like that. Would you mind if I spent about an hour scanning the ground?" He said, "Na, that's ok, go ahead, but ya won't find much." I replied, "Thanks a lot, you're probably right, but it sure beats working!" Ha!" He smiled and returned to plowing his field! I was shocked and happier than an Eskimo rubbing noses.

When I was done searching his property, I had found three musket balls, some leather shoe parts and two revolutionary war buttons. I returned later that day with a freshly made blueberry pie to give to him as my way of thanking him for being so kind and granting me permission to search his land. I knew that I would be back again in the future so I wanted to be sure he remembered me and, of course, that delicious blueberry pie.

Gettysburg and My Friend Dan

As a Northeastern Regional Sales Manager, I had a representative working for me by the name of Dan. Great guy! Dan lived close to Gettysburg, PA and he suggested that I hunt his land. He said he had heard that the troops had crossed his land on their way to Gettysburg and that his land was once owned by William Penn. You can imagine all of the thoughts that ran through my mind and, of course, I couldn't wait to take him up on his offer and search his property!

I arrived at Dan's by 6:00 PM. There was still plenty of daylight left on that summer day, so I took my detector and started searching. Since his land had been recently plowed, I figured I'd start right behind his house. With his kids watching closely, I began to walk on the plowed area and got within about twenty feet and there, on top of the ground, lay a large coin! No need to even dig since it was right there in plain sight. It turned out to be a large Connecticut copper penny!

Imagine the excitement we all felt when we examined the coin! I think that particular moment gave them the impression that metal detecting was an easy activity. Ha, not a chance. However, after several hours that day and all through the next, I located two more coins and various Civil War related relics. It was a very nice visit spending time with my colleague Dan and his family! A wonderful stay, dinner and conversation! Truly, a great family.

Shortly afterward, I gathered all the items I had found and put them in a shadow box and presented it to Dan and his lovely family. They hung it above their fireplace. I felt so fortunate to have had the chance to spend this time with Dan, for soon after, Dan developed cancer at the young age of 54 and passed away. Once again, metal detecting had proven to be so much more than just finding tangible treasures! It also creates priceless memories to share with others along with a message to enjoy the moments not the days!

Land or Water Searches?

Many people ask me, what's the best place to search? Land or water? I reply that it all depends on what's available for you locally or how far you're willing to travel. Also, which one do you really enjoy doing? It also depends on what type of physical shape you're currently in. Each type of search can be very demanding on your body. Land searches require a tremendous amount of bending down and getting back up again. They also require digging hard soil and cutting through roots, using a lot of wrist and upper body strength. Water searches require long periods of time wading in water with unknown obstacles below the surface. In addition, water searches require the use of a long handled metal scoop that weighs quite a bit, especially when it's filled with mud. Bringing that scoop full of mud to the surface, even in the water, can be quite a chore for someone not very strong.

Tip #18: *It pays big dividends to be as active as possible and to work out lightly with weights prior to getting involved with metal detecting. Conditioning your entire body, however so slightly, helps you live a healthier and more active life in general. You'll have more enjoyment while treasure hunting (and just living your daily life) with no aches and pains.*

I'm currently a registered 3rd degree Black Belt in traditional Japanese Karate, hence, the weekly training keeps me in decent shape for all types of detecting. I have different kinds of pain related to practicing martial arts, however, that's my own choice, so no complaints from this peanut gallery!

Do yourself a favor and, regardless of what age you presently are, get used to some form of daily exercise, even if it's just walking. Keep yourself active in any way you can, but keep it enjoyable and realistic. Don't stress yourself out. Choose an exercise that you can be comfortable doing and that does not cause you difficulty in breathing.

Personally, I like searching both land and water and I have been very successful with each.

Tip #19: *Get to know your detector, believe in yourself and your own capabilities, and you'll never get skunked! I have never gone treasure hunting without finding something, even it's been just trash. I have always discovered something and you will too!*

However, since I'm claustrophobic, I'm not able to scuba dive, which limits me to searches in water no deeper than five feet. That's one reason I concentrate on shallow water searches.

If I could ever cure myself of my phobia, I would love to learn how to scuba dive. The opportunities are endless. Searching where most people cannot gain access is exciting and the rewards are unlimited. However, until then, I'll continue searching in the shallow water swim areas. They have yielded some pretty nice treasures along the way!

Land search pros: Easier access, are less complicated (water searches tend to be more physically demanding and require additional specialized equipment), and less preparation required prior to searching. Many more locations are available and you can search at a moment's notice. I always carry my detector in my vehicle at all times. You never know when you might come across an area that has just been dug up, is under construction, or is being repaired, that could yield treasure before that area is once again unavailable to search!

Even the smallest area can be searched and you never know what lays beneath the surface. The soil you currently see could have come from far away, perhaps during the construction of the area, and brought with it coin and jewelry from a different era! I've actually found foreign coins in my garden mulch....without my detector. How they got there is anyone's guess. I was totally shocked. Never underestimate the potential treasure laying just below the surface you're currently standing on!

Land search cons: You must always be careful when digging and understand the capability of the type of digging tool you are using. For example, if it's a shovel you're using, you have underground cables to be concerned about. Sometimes, they may not necessarily be buried as deep as local code mandates, therefore, they are much closer to the surface than you would imagine and very easy to cut.

Have a feel for the land area that you're about to dig with any tool. Rural areas have their own set of dangers. Uncapped hand dug wells, old foundations, sinkholes, wires and cables, sharp objects, rusty targets, bottle tops with broken glass attached facing upward as you dig downward, just to name a few. Use common sense when you're treasure hunting. If the area you are searching is unknown to you, approach every step with caution and care.

Tip #20: *Get yourself a box of surgical latex gloves at a big box store for about $8, and <u>wear them</u>! They give you protection against any unknown chemicals or rash generating plants in the ground. When was the last* time you had a tetanus shot? Also, remember that animal feces takes a long time to biodegrade. Get my message? Better to be safe than sorry!

Remember, dry soil is much harder to recover targets from than moist soil. On the other hand, your detector conducts signals better in the moist soil than dry soil since it uses the moisture to detect deeper targets. I have discovered that I have much better luck searching during or right after a rain shower. Messy? Yes, but the rewards seem to be better, too, and worth the effort.

Tip # 21: Once you've located a target with the large coil on your detector, use your probe to narrow the dig area needed to recover the target. Place a small piece of cloth or paper towel next to the hole to lay your soil on and cut a small circular plug around the target area. Gently lift the plug and lay it on the cloth or paper towel. If done correctly, your treasure should be within the plug itself or directly below in the hole. Replace the soil and tamp down the area you just dug. Make it so no one can see where you just dug. You should walk away knowing that squirrels make more of a mess than you do when you search for your target.

Tip #22-A: Always be sure to clean your detector when you arrive back home. A good rinse of the coil with clean water is all it takes to keep your detector in nice working condition. Check your detector model handbook for care of your detector and follow the suggestions. Taking care of your detector will give you years of enjoyment!

#22-B: I know this sounds strange but you must be careful not to cut yourself while recovering your target. Always carry band aids with you for this very reason. You don't think it can happen? Trust me, even *the best of us cut ourselves recovering treasure. It's not a matter of IF it will happen, but a matter of WHEN it will happen, so be prepared.*

#22-C: I find it best to carry my digging tool on my belt on my side and a pouch (small fanny pack) in front of me on the same belt. These are always together in my car along with my detector ready to search an area.

Tip # 23: *Always let someone know where you'll be detecting and what time to expect you to return. I know this sounds childish but in reality, if you're like me, you'll venture into areas most people would not go, including areas with no cell phone service. As a result, you need to be prepared to face any situation that would affect your health and wellbeing. As a hunter and someone who loves the outdoors, I have taken Search and Rescue Courses and I am a Master Bow Hunting Instructor for the State of New York, hence, I have a lot of survival background to rely on when needed.*

Side bar note here: Recently, I had a feeling of discomfort in my chest area for about a week. I told my wife about it and we said we'd keep an eye on it. We agreed to get it checked if it felt any worse. No pain, just some vague discomfort similar to the feeling of swallowing food that didn't quite make it down to the stomach that stayed in the upper throat area.

Around that time on a Sunday evening as the sun was setting and the temperature was unusually warm for a late November day, I told my wife I was going to capture what little sun there was left to search an area around a local older home that I had been given permission to hunt. I told her I shouldn't be more than an hour.

As I walked to the car, I checked the battery in my phone and realized that it was extremely low. I realized I would have no way to call anyone should anything happen while I was detecting. Being so excited about being able to search so late in the year, combined with the fact that the property I was headed for was built early in the 1800's, you can imagine the thoughts of what treasure I could possibly find was going through my head at that time.

But sound reasoning was about to take over. As much as I wanted to get there and start searching, something told me to go back in the house and get the discomfort in my chest checked out at the local hospital emergency room. So, reluctantly I returned to the house and told my wife that we should probably go to the hospital just to be sure nothing was wrong.

I had everything checked out. Chest x-ray, two sets of cardiac enzymes and an EKG all tested negative for any problem. I was told it was probably a mild case of pneumonia. They gave me some medication and then sent me home.

After a rough night, the next morning I was still feeling the discomfort, but not real pain as I entered my shower. As I was drying off, the discomfort abruptly changed to extreme chest pain and I had a tough time making it back to the bedroom. My wife, (a former cardiac perfusionist that worked on a heart transplant team) knew exactly what was taking place and called 911. I was having a massive heart attack!

As a 3rd degree black belt and having trained most of my life, I have always tried to be physically fit in every way possible. I had no past history of any illness specifically related to the heart except an irregular

60

heart beat that had been corrected in the past, and here I was doubled over in excruciating chest pain that turned out to be 100% blockage in one of my arteries.

My life was saved by the awareness of my wife and an ambulance trip to the hospital emergency room while in excruciating cardiac pain. I was rushed to the cath lab where a stent was inserted to open the 100% blockage that I had in one of my coronary arteries. I was thankful that it was caught in time, or I wouldn't be here writing this book that you're now reading!

It turns out that I have a family history of coronary artery disease that I wasn't aware of at the time. After four additional stents placed a month later, for a total of five, I feel fantastic! Thanks to everyone involved, I have a new lease on life.

Tip #24:

Always listen to what your body is telling you and don't brush off any discomfort that you may have, especially in the chest area. Metal detecting is a physically demanding activity and it can stress your body in ways that other activities don't. It's so much more than just grabbing a detector and heading out the door. It requires careful thought and planning beforehand to prevent a tragedy. Can you imagine if the desire to detect had prevented me from thinking rationally that Sunday evening and I had ventured out with a dead cell phone battery? I would have ended up just like that battery!

Land searches can yield some nice treasure and, if done correctly, your metal detecting experience can create a lot of nice memories and stories to tell your kids and grandkids as the years pass on! Even in this world of instant gratification and technological wonder, stories of finding treasure of all kinds are stories most children (and adults) enjoy hearing from a friend or loved one!

The excitement created never ceases to amaze me when I hear the many questions asked by those looking over my collection of jewelry, coins, and artifacts. "Holy cow! You found all this?" "Where did you find it?" "How long did it take you?" "What's the most unusual thing you've ever found?" "What's the most expensive thing you've ever found?" These and a countless number of other questions are commonly asked.

I love to watch as they look through my "Box of Tears" of jewelry and the infinite amount of clad coins, new and old, and yes, even the worthless junk that I've saved. This demonstrates to everyone that metal detecting isn't always about finding expensive treasure, but also a journey beneath the surface of the ground to capture the lost items of humans before us and the memories created while searching.

Land searching opens the door to countless treasure and items that make you wonder how they got lost in the first place? How did they end up where you found them and, better yet, why so deep in the ground that seems so dense and hard?

Over time, nature and gravity have a way of pulling everything downward and, with additional pressure from above, all that is dropped upon the ground continues to go deeper and deeper. Gone undetected (no pun intended) items, over time, settle below the surface. They are just waiting for you and I to find them and bring them back to our life today. I always wonder about the history of every single target I discover and relish the fact that I now touch an object not seen or touched by another human being for years and years!

Land searches at night present their own set of circumstances and rewards not related to daytime searches. There's a whole lot of things to be concerned about and to watch out for that are much different than daytime searches!

Tip # 25: *Make sure that you know where you're searching at night and that you pose no security risk while doing so! Wandering around land with a long thing in your hand pointed to the ground can easily be mistaken for someone with a rifle! I don't suggest night searching unless you are on private land and everyone knows who you are and what you are doing! Let common sense prevail here!*

The same common sense should be used while searching wooded areas during any hunting season! Be extremely aware of the hunting regulation dates in your area before wandering around the forest looking for relics. Hunters, as cautious as they usually are, can mistakenly think a distant figure dressed in brown slowly wandering around with a long light colored handle is a possible deer, with antlers browsing. The last thing a hunter would even expect to see would be some person metal detecting in the woods during hunting season!

Nighttime searches would seem to have an advantage. Less people questioning you and more peaceful with less interruptions. Still, night searches are certainly more risky and dangerous and I would advise against it. No treasure is worth losing a limb or your life over, not to mention the nocturnal animals that feed at night and have no problem letting you know that they are in the same area. One animal in particular has the ability to leave an impression on you in a hideous manner that you'll never forget. A "black cat" with a white stripe down its back also known as the skunk! Phew!

Shallow Water Searches

Metal detecting in shallow water is a whole different ballgame. Unlike scuba diving, shallow water searches can be conducted in fresh water, ocean water or any body of water that doesn't go over your head. Usually searches are done in water that's only 4-5 feet deep.

Sound strange? It is. But think about it for a minute. Most bathers do most of their activity in shallow water, activities such as throwing footballs, Frisbees or just horsing around with their friends. You'll also see parents with their children, people standing around getting cooled off while they enjoy their drinks, and usually, local boaters anchored in the shallow water just hanging out on the boat while their passengers are frolicking around in the water. These are just a few examples of how hundreds and literally thousands of people congregate in the shallow water area all over the world!

Now what happens to our fingers when we spend a lot of time in the water? They shrink. While our fingers are shrinking, the gold and silver jewelry is expanding in the sun. This together with the physical activity is the perfect combination that continually refills the underwater floor with countless treasures!

Yes, it's sad that people lose their jewelry while they're in the water, but if God didn't allow that to happen, then shallow water metal detecting wouldn't exist! Ha, just kidding, but really, every treasure I've found has been the result of someone losing it and how that happened is something I think about all the time! I would love to know the exact circumstances surrounding the loss. It's amazing to me how that treasure has been waiting there for me to come along in the future and discover it! Just imagine dropping something in the water, and then it lays there for over 50-60 or even hundreds of years until a person with a metal detector comes along to discover it! Mind boggling.

Here's what I always say to the people in the water who wade up to me and ask, "Hey, what are you looking for?" I smile and say, "Stay in school and get a good education so you won't have to do this later in life, but seriously....don't wear jewelry in the water!" Then they realize what I'm _really_ saying and always look at their ring finger to see if their ring is still on their hand.

Tip #26: *If you decide to water search in and around bathers while they are in the water, then you need to be prepared to encounter all types of people; curiosity seekers, kidders, wise guys, seniors, little kids, and people who don't know or understand what it is that you're doing. Sometimes, it's simply that they don't like you being around them metal detecting while they're in the water!*

To me, it's really odd how a few individuals can have such a strange and negative attitude toward another person in the water simply enjoying an activity that they themselves are not familiar with. Especially metal detecting. This is something I have never figured out, nor do I care to waste my time even thinking about it. For the most part, the majority of people will not bother you in a negative way, however, for the few that do, it can be an unenjoyable experience. Just be prepared to experience those kind of moments whenever you're metal detecting on the land or in the water. It's not IF it'll happen, but WHEN it'll happen!

So if you're going to shallow water detect, you'll have to toughen up your skin, your mind, and keep a positive outlook. Don't forget, when someone meets a person metal detecting for the first time, they will undoubtedly keep that impression forever, so it needs to be a positive experience. Then the next time they encounter a detectorist, they'll feel the same way and treat that person accordingly.

Tip #27: *Respect fellow detectorists and the people who ask you many questions. Give them the same courtesy you would like to be shown.*

Shallow water searching hints: One bonus of shallow water hunts is the fact that usually, the treasures that you find are usually in pretty good shape, depending on how long they've been in the water and, if the water is fresh or salt water.

I want you to picture a scenario that I have found myself in hundreds of times. You're in your shorty wet suit (because you're going to be in the water for several hours) and you have your long handled, aluminum water scoop with you that will help you retrieve your targets. You are wading through the water as everyone else is frolicking about. They are unaware of what you are really doing as you wade past them. Oh, they see your headphones but they figure you're just a person who's not bothering anyone and going about your water sport as they are enjoying theirs. They have no idea that the treasure you are searching for is valuable and sometimes very expensive gold or silver jewelry that can be returned, saved, or redeemed for thousands of dollars! No one has a clue that you have spent countless hours preparing for these searching expeditions or know the expenses associated with the sport of metal detecting.

They don't have a clue of how exciting this activity can actually be nor do they really care. Metal detecting isn't for everyone and you realize that fact as you continue to slowly wade about in the water. Above the surface they see you with your hat, headphones and usually sunglasses on, but they cannot see the long handled scoop or the actual metal detector that you're searching with below the surface.

Suddenly, your detector sends you a strong signal that it has located metal in the soil beneath you! You swing your coil back and forth over the target trying to determine the target's exact location since you can't actually see it below the water. The signal is sometimes strong and then it's weak. You ask yourself, what's up with that? How can that be? The technique with which you swing your coil over the target can have a profound effect on how quickly you locate the target. The closer and more level you keep your coil to the seabed floor, will usually mean a better signal. If you swing higher, then you are obviously much farther from the target and the signal will be weak and or variable.

Tip #28: *It doesn't matter if you're land or water searching, you must be swinging the coil properly to obtain the best results. Always swing level with the ground in a complete pass in front of you. By that I mean, don't swing like I sometimes see a novice detectorist do, seasoned ones as well, and swing the coil in an upward curve at the end of each pass. Keep the coil level to the ground at all times from left to right and go slowly! You will find more treasure and have better results!*

If you are right handed, follow these guidelines, reverse if you are left handed. Once you've narrowed the signal to a specific location under the water, take your detector and place the coil on the seabed floor directly on top of your target. Next place the big toe of your right foot up against the edge of the coil closest to you which is now laying on top of your target. As you lift and move your metal detector off to the side of your body, (don't worry, it'll remain attached to your body by the headphone cord) place the point of the long handled water scoop that's in your left hand at the same spot of where your big toe was and then place your right foot on top of the water scoop. Apply pressure downward sending the scoop, hopefully, deep under your target.

At this point, you're digging your first scoop downward, in and under your target. Once your scoop has reached as deep as it can go, pull the handle of the scoop backward which should place your target right in the center of your scoop. Then slide your left hand down the handle until it's close to the scoop itself. This will give you better leverage to start raising the scoop upward. Finally, lift the scoop up from the bottom of the seabed floor. It will be full of sand and also heavy, so be careful to keep it level at all times. At this point you have a choice.

With your detector dangling on your side in the water attached by your headphone cord, take your right hand, and, while keeping the scoop under the water in your left hand, slowly and carefully feel through the sand that's in the scoop. You'll then be able to locate the hidden treasure within your scoop that you fought so hard to bring to the surface!

Tip #29: *Caution! Since you have no idea what dangerous items could be within your scoop, you must be careful as you feel your way through the sand and or mud. Sharp objects could be in the scoop and you could cut your fingers without even knowing it until you bring your hand out of the water! Or, worse yet, the target could be an old rusty object that could cause injury to your fingers and require you to have a tetanus shot. You must be slow and methodical anytime you place your hand in your scoop!*

As you feel your way within the scoop with your fingers, tilt the scoop on an angle so that the target finds its way to the side and bottom of the scoop. This will make it much easier to locate. There is a special rush that will come over you as your fingers sift through the sand and you actually feel the target! Feeling the target with your fingers while it's still in the scoop but out of sight, can give you a strong visual inside your brain. You'll want to savor those special moments for those are the exact moments that all detectorists hope to experience. Discovering that the target you just retrieved actually turns out to be a beautiful piece of jewelry or another object of great interest or value.

Once located, the target takes on new meaning. First, it means that your search has paid off. Secondly, it means that you have touched something that has been under the water for who knows how long as you are trying to figure out what it actually is that you are now touching in your scoop!

With your mind going crazy with excitement, your fingers might feel a round item with a hole in the center and a small attachment on the top center of the target. It feels like a ring. You might actually feel the diamond on top! Wow! That target could turn out to be a valuable ring. In fact, you could swear you actually feel the diamond as you pass your fingers over the top!

Your imagination is now going wild. You're thinking at this point that your first underwater target could actually turn out to be a ring! So, you slowly take it out of the scoop. You're being extra careful not to drop it back into the water as you raise it up to see it in the sunlight.

When it reaches the surface in your fingers, the sun hits it and you see a beautiful silver object glistening in the sunlight. As you bring it closer to your eyes, you realize that what you were just visualizing in your mind is not exactly what you're holding. It turns out to be a small decorative part from a boat that holds the rope along the bow. Crap!

That nice rush you were feeling quickly leaves your mind and disappointment sets in immediately! What the %$#$%???? How can this be? It felt like a ring. It seemed to be a ring and you could actually feel it. A boat part? What???

Tip #30: *Remember "why" you are detecting. It's not always about the treasure, but rather all of the enjoyment that comes along with metal detecting in general. The air, the water, the wind on your face, and the enjoyment of just being active and outside, living life to its fullest. Sure, you're disappointed but that only lasts for a moment and you know deep down that the target you finally found, COULD have been a ring! That's enough reason to continue searching for your next target!*

Tip #31: *Remember, it only takes <u>one ring</u> to pay for a treasure hunt!* With the high price of gold and silver, finding a ring of either metal can reward you nicely and make the entire treasure search an experience to remember. I've searched for hours on end only to find trash and other useless junk and, not until I was on my way back, did I finally come across a terrific find!

Tip #32: _Never give up! Sometimes, it's the very last key on the key ring that unlocks the lock! Many nice treasures have been found as I continued to search while leaving the water and headed back to shore!_

The other choice you have after you have located the target and you think you have it in your scoop is to bring the level scoop to the surface of the water and move it back and forth, allowing the water itself to wash away the sand or mud inside the scoop to reveal your treasure.

As you watch the sand filter out the holes of your scoop with each back and forth movement, you will see the soil amount decrease as it gets closer to the bottom but you still aren't actually able to SEE the target. You may begin to think that maybe you didn't actually get the target in your scoop. Don't despair as it certainly may be there. Many a coin has laid against the side of the scoop or flat on the bottom of the scoop and ended up back into the water due to an over anxious detectorist.

Tip #33: _It is a good idea to install a small round magnet in the bottom center of your scoop. The magnet will catch useless items such as bobby pins, nails, bottle caps, pieces of scrap metal, and all ferrous (metal containing iron) items._

Concentrate on the bottom of the scoop until ALL the water has finally left the scoop. Carefully scan the entire scoop for any coins that may have stuck to the side. I have found many coins doing just that! When you notice the coin in the bottom of your scoop, try and imagine what kind of coin it may be. Is it an old coin or newer coin, or, is it one that you've never seen before? Let these thoughts go through your head as you reach down and grab the coin. I have found coins with 13 stars around the border which immediately told me that the coin was from an era when the United States had only the 13 original colonies! You never know what you're going to find when treasure hunting so let your mind explore the various possibilities of what your target could be until you actually touch the target itself.

Imagine for a moment now that your scoop is holding the target somewhere in the soil in your scoop. You are now moving it back and forth, forcing the soil out through the holes in the side and bottom of your scoop. As the soil gets closer to the bottom, you notice a shiny round object with a hole in the center and it actually turns out to be a ring!!!!!

The feeling that you're going to feel at that particular moment is unreal! Especially when it's your *first* ring! A ring of any kind is so exciting to find! You're finding something that someone had once purchased or was given as a gift, and somehow it found itself in the sand at the bottom of a body of water. Now, years later you come along and discover it. How exciting!

If someone said to you that they'd give you a million dollars to wade out into the water and find the ring that they just lost in the water, it would be next to impossible. Yet, through the process of shallow water searching, I have found the smallest of rings, earrings, nose rings, toe rings, bracelets, tie tacks, and diamond studded earrings just by wading in the water! You can too!

Attempting to find a specific piece of jewelry that has *just* been lost in the water, is next to impossible because there so many variables that can affect the outcome. Tides, currents, depth, density of sand or mud on the water's bottom just to name a few.

However, always give it a try for someone who has just lost a sentimental piece of jewelry in the hopes that you can recover it for them. Show them that, as a detectorist, you too have a heart, and your attempt to find their lost item proves just that. If you're lucky enough to find it, great! If not, then at least you tried. It's a memorable moment for everyone involved.

A Woman's Cry for Help

I was laying on the sand on my blanket catching some rays at the beach with my detector and equipment leaning against the tent, when my wife came running up to me from the water and shouted to me, "Honey, someone just lost their engagement ring! Can you come quickly and look for it with your detector?" Of course I would and quickly got my gear and ran to the water's edge.

There in the ocean surf in the waves was a group of people looking downward as they waded about looking for the young lady's engagement ring. She was so distraught, but since she had just lost it, I was confident I could locate it. It seemed to give her some small relief that the guy with the equipment could actually find her ring.

I immediately went to the area where she said she had been standing in the water when she lost it and searched for an hour to no avail. The ocean has a way of gulping up lost items with waves and undercurrents and, even though I was, so to speak, a "Johnny on the Spot" with all my great looking detector gear, in the end it didn't matter. Her ring was nowhere to be found. At least for that day and at that time anyway.

I returned time and time again over my vacation that week and I never did find her ring, but in the meantime, while searching for her ring, I found several other nice rings and several coins. I believe in Karma, good and bad. Do good things for others and good things will happen to you along the way!

The point being that, despite being right there at the time that her ring was lost, I could not find it. The ocean can be kind one day and harsh the next. I felt bad but I took her name and number and assured her that, as a man of my word, if I ever found her engagement ring I would return it back to her!

Ocean shallow water detecting requires you to be more aware of your surroundings, even more than fresh water! One must use common sense.

Tip #34: *Common sense is NOT always common knowledge!*

Wading out into the ocean surf could result in encountering of the following dangerous situations: rip tides, deep holes on the ocean floor, crashing waves, salt water that burns your eyes and leaves your equipment sticky, ocean creatures that sting, bite, and can grab onto you, jelly fish, sand sharks, and soft squishy sand at the bottom are just a few of the hazards when considering whether to metal detect in the ocean!

Another issue to consider is that the ocean is not always your friend. The waves will constantly smash up against you. The strong ocean current will lift you and throw you around like a human bobber in the water. It's extremely difficult to retrieve a target in the crashing waves once you've located a target. As you try and place your scoop at the underwater signal that you've found, the waves will smash you and take your long handled scoop right out of your hand and, once that happens, you end up looking for your scoop and not the signal!

The ocean constantly tries your patience and, if you don't have much patience to begin with, you should think twice about detecting in the ocean.

Do you ever wonder why you don't see many detectorists actually searching out in the ocean surf? The reasons that I've mentioned above are just a few reasons why most detectorists stay up on the soft sand of the beach or stay in the hard pan area just down to the water's edge.

To detect in the ocean, remember, you'll need to be in the best physical shape that you can be and have the confidence to address any dangerous situation that arises. It is best to always have someone nearby that's aware you are in the water metal detecting. Never search alone.

Having said all the above, there are times when the ocean can be calm and the water is not as dangerous. If you are in a bay area where the wind is not a factor, then you'll have less waves. If you are in a large resort area, and the beach area has a long shallow swim area, then there's less chance of having the underwater hazards I mentioned.

There are ocean areas that you can search in at the same time that swimmers and surfers are also enjoying their sport. This gives you some hope that someone is usually watching what you're doing and, should you run into a problem, someone could call for help. In some cases there's even a lifeguard on duty who will also be keeping an eye on you.

Regardless of fresh or salt water shallow water searching, I can't stress enough to use common sense! If you feel the least bit uncomfortable doing it, then listen to your instincts, don't go into the water and stay on the outside edge. Here's several ways to have a safe and enjoyable experience searching the ocean water....

Tip #35: *Check the tide charts. These are available free on line. Check the area that you're planning to be searching in and look for the low tide time schedule. Plan your search to be in the shallow water (knee to waist deep only) at that time. This will position you to be the farthest out from shore that you can go without actually using scuba gear. This is the area that should put you into several ocean "cuts" (underwater groves where the current catches treasure from shifting any farther out to sea). Finding one of the cuts will give you the best chance of finding lots of lost items that have gathered in the lower underwater area. If you are out far enough at low tide, you'll be in an area that very few detectorists venture into and the odds are much better of finding nice treasure that's usually out of reach for most detectorists. But I must repeat, if water searches were that easy, then everybody would be doing it!*

Tip #36: *Search perpendicular to the shoreline while keeping an eye on the shore at all times. Take each step slowly, keeping your coil just above the ocean floor. Be sure that everything you are carrying on your waist belt is secured. With each pass, waves have a tendency to grab things that are loose and take them out to sea never to be found again.*

The farther out you go, the bigger the waves become. Carry your important papers, such as your driver's license or ID in a watertight bag that you can put under your hat on top of your head that's secured by your headphones.

Wear plenty of sun block on the back of your neck, your face, your lips, and the tops of your ears. The water tends to attract more sunlight and the reflection off the water can cause severe sunburn. They make hats that have a piece of cloth that dangles off the back to protect your neck should you decide to wear one. You can find these hats online or at most sporting goods stores.

Be careful when reaching into your water scoop to retrieve a target. The scoop can contain sea creatures like crabs and jellyfish that can wreak havoc for you.

Whenever you're planning to be in ocean water that is cold like in the New England Atlantic area, be sure to wear at least a "shorty" wet suit. Regardless of how hot the air temperature is, remember, the ocean water temperature is usually colder, and all the time you spend searching could cause you to possibly get hypothermia. Once your body gets cold in the water, it's difficult to get warm again unless you completely come out of the water and return to shore. Also, your skin becomes "prune-like" and you can lose your own jewelry unless you're wearing gloves. I find all of my water searching gear at dive shops. They always have lots of close-outs and special sales that you can take advantage of.

As you can see, there are a lot of things to be concerned about when you decide to go shallow water metal detecting in the ocean. I know it may sound hard to believe, but everything I have mentioned here becomes a stark reality when you actually begin searching. I have saved you a lot of aggravation by helping you avoid many pitfalls that would've made your shallow water metal detecting experience an uncomfortable and, worst yet, possibly even a dangerous one.

Tip #37: *Remember the five P's...Proper Planning Prevents Poor Programs!* An old cliché but definitely true, and it applies to many facets of life in general.

Fresh water searches can be safe, enjoyable and very rewarding if you follow the same guidelines and preparation as for ocean water searching. Local swimming holes have their own set of circumstances that vary from location to location and you must be aware of these hazards at all times while venturing into the water.

If you're like me, you'll want to find old swimming holes that haven't been used in years, and you can imagine the unusual items that you might find. Also, remember that time has a way of creating hazards that weren't there back in the day when swimmers were using the water, so keep in mind all of the possible things that could go wrong while you're out there wading in shallow water.

Unknown things like ledges and drop offs can appear quickly. Be sure to always wade slowly and use your coil as a guide in front of you just as a blind person uses a pointer. Your coil will tell you if the ground in front of you is uneven, deeper, or if there are objects hidden from view that you would be stepping on or tripping over, or even worse yet, getting your foot tangled in.

I have only read of one shallow water detectorist drowning while shallow water searching. Apparently, he slipped off a hidden ledge and, without knowing the exact details, I would venture to think that he probably tried holding on to his equipment when he slipped since he was probably startled. Regardless, it was a tragedy for him and his family and friends.

Just like anything in life, you have to be aware of your surroundings and always consider the "what if" scenario as you go about your sport. That way, should anything happen, your reaction can make the difference between life and death for you and others around you. Don't think it can't happen to you! (Famous last words eh?)

Old swimming holes contain a ton of trash and items you may not have thought of such as sinkers, barbed fish hooks, anchors, and boat deck materials such as clamps. Also, knives, nuts and bolts, fishing lures, logs and branches, cans, bottles, glass jars and lids of jars with jagged, broken glass attached.

Sometimes, people target shoot at bottles floating near the shore and, when the bottles are hit with a bullet, the glass breaks and the remaining part of the jar with the lid falls to the bottom with some of the glass jar still attached. This leaves jagged edges facing upward toward the surface waiting for someone to step on.

Tip #38: *When metal detecting in ANY body of water, fresh or salt water, always wear water foot covers. Never go barefoot! Save yourself an accident by being prepared ahead of time.*

I have stepped on, been tangled in, stuck by, cut by, and caught in all sorts of items below the surface. One never knows what lies in wait for you when you enter a swimming area. I am always amazed at the swimmers who are totally clueless to the hazards below the surface and yet I see them every time without any protective foot wear while I'm shallow water searching.

I think to myself, if they only knew. But then again, it probably wouldn't make any difference. That's one reason I always wear water socks or something similar on my feet whenever I enter the water.

Three Kids in Danger

It was a windy but very sunny and warm day at a local public swimming area. I was enjoying the fact that I was not working, but instead, I was searching about in the shallow water finding coins and jewelry. As I waded about detecting, I noticed three young children, somewhere around the ages of about four to ten, with swim bubbles on their arms and small inflatables around their waists, wading out into the water.

They came close to me trying to figure out what I was doing and I gave them a smile as they passed me by in their protective water gear. I wondered that, since they had all this protective gear that, they must not be able to swim. I also thought that they must have parents or a guardian close by. I looked around and didn't see anyone except for a couple laying on the beach about 60 yards away.

The water was swift and one foot waves were crashing from the wind, but that didn't cause any problem for me. As for the kids, well, they loved it and waded from sand bar to sand bar on their journey outward.

As a typical parent, I kept an occasional eye on them when, suddenly, I hit a strong signal. It sounded like gold so I concentrated on getting the target and took my eyes off the three children. As I was digging with my scoop and bouncing around in the water, I saw several of the inflatables that the girls had been wearing float by me. I looked over at the girls and they were waving their hands in desperation. They were standing on a sandbar and the waves had taken away their protection. I realized how serious the situation was so I stopped digging, gathered the inflatables and waded out to the girls.

Being tall has its advantages while shallow water detecting and this was definitely one time my 6 ft. height really paid off! I was able to get to the girls, give them their inflatable protection back, and accompany them back to the shore where their parents were asleep basking in the sun, totally unaware of how dangerous the situation was at the time.

Having done my good deed for the day, I headed back out to try to locate that strong target I had found but, even as experienced as I am at metal detecting, I was unable to find it again. It would have to wait for another day or for another detectorist to retrieve the hidden treasure, however, I was comfortable with the fact that saving three beautiful little girls from a possible drowning was much more rewarding than finding any treasure!

The day turned out to be pretty good anyway and I left the water with about three dollars in coin, two rings, one silver the other gold, and a bunch of trash. Not a bad hunt at all!

Personally, I have found that swimmers, usually it's the young teenage boys who are "feeling their oats" and who have a tendency to be more outgoing than others, don't hesitate to come up and ask me directly what I'm doing. In several cases, when they think I'm not aware of them and that I can't possibly hear them with the headphones on my ears, they make rude comments to me and, when they do, I simply ignore them and they usually go away. However, with the more aggressive teenagers, I've had them throw mud balls and things at me while trying to be funny with their friends. When I address the situation with them it's not long before they realize I don't stand for that and usually I can downplay everything so we all have a good time. Being a third degree Black Belt has its advantages.

Teenage Jet Skier Down

Talk about obnoxious! When you're shallow water searching around other people who are also enjoying the water, situations can turn ugly quickly. Especially when you enter a drunken teenager on a powerful jet ski. As I continued detecting, the Jet Skier, who was about 60 yards farther out from me, carried on for about 40 minutes showing off for his friends back on shore. He was doing flips, doughnuts and other acrobatics over and over again until finally, one of his stunts tossed him clear off the Jet Ski and into the water! I watched him close to see if he was able to swim and to be sure that he wasn't injured. He could indeed swim and wasn't hurt but probably was embarrassed. I watched his Jet Ski float right by me and could hear him swearing his head off, very upset! Oh, I could have reached out and grabbed the jet-ski and returned it to him, but I thought this would be a good time for him to learn some humility, so I let it pass me by and it finally ended up on the shore.

A couple who also heard his antics and thought he was actually drowning waded frantically out against the waves to reach him and when they did, he started swearing at them. That made them turn around and wade back to shore in disgust! After all, here they were trying to do a good deed, but his vanity got the best of him and he told them to back off. He would swim to shore himself, and so he did.

It gave me great pleasure to watch a life lesson take place in front of me, all the while knowing that no one was in any danger. Truly, a parent's gift and only another parent would understand why I didn't intervene in the first place.

Tip #39: *Some of life's best learned lessons come from the worst experiences!*

Permits Needed to Detect

There are certain swim areas and local beaches that are run by the state and they have several restrictions on WHEN, WHERE and HOW you can metal detect. It's very important to find out the details *before* you begin your searches. Usually, but not always, there's a minor fee for the permit application and the application must be filed by a certain time for it to be granted. Check with your local state and town laws. They will have all the information you need.

Tip #40: *Always ask permission! Why put yourself at risk for a fine or, worse yet, an arrest while attempting to enjoy an activity you really like? Simply put, no treasure is worth it!*

Sometimes, even when you HAVE a permit, you can find yourself in precarious situations through no fault of your own. People who have a little authority sometimes have a habit of exercising that authority just because they can. As a result, depending on your personality and, you can find yourself in the middle of an unpleasant situation.

Every person has a unique personality and, when you're interacting with them, your disposition can affect the way they treat you. Having been in sales and marketing all my life I have come to understand that philosophy and, if possible, try very hard NOT to offend anyone along the way. However, as I have explained to my children, if you believe in something and you find yourself being challenged on that subject, then stand your ground and defend your belief. Have an open mind but support your thoughts with facts and not just with hearsay. Keep your voice down, stay calm and state your facts. Usually, that is enough to show the other person that you know what you're talking about and they'll usually understand.

"Outta of the Water NOW"

Those are the words that I heard when I was told by a local park employee to show him my valid metal detecting permit that authorized me to be in the water of that swimming area at that time.

He was part of the park cleanup crew and they were cleaning the beach area the day after the Labor Day holiday which, in the New England area, is the last day to be at the beach enjoying yourself before school begins. As a result, there's a ton of litter left behind from the beachgoers.

The permit that I had is valid only from the morning of the day AFTER Labor Day. It remains good for only the next several months, however, the winter sets in quickly and makes metal detecting difficult at best and non-existent in the New England area until spring time. As a result I take metal detecting in this area on this day very seriously and look forward to it each year. Traveling over 300 miles round trip to enjoy searching this particular state park. Also, I meet my brother Fred every year at the park at that time. It has become the special place where we get together once a year, barring no health issues. We can count on seeing each other at 5:00 AM, same spot, same time year after year. It has become a ritual of sorts, and there are other detectorists who join us. At that time, we are all part of an event that creates new memories, and we share past stories of our metal detecting experiences throughout the year! It is a nice feeling to see the same people year after year. They are part of a metal detecting fraternity that gathers around local swim areas each year for just a short time, yet, are close enough to hear about family members and how each of our lives have been going. Always friendly, sincere, endearing, and with lots of laughter we share what's happened in each of our lives over the past year.

One such person was a school coach by the name of Dan. Dan told us one year that we probably wouldn't see him again the next year because he had been diagnosed with brain cancer and wasn't expected to live much longer. Our hearts sank in disbelief that his story could be true and we all discussed the positive side of life with him, giving him hope and support, and telling him that miracles do happen, so don't give up. Fight it all the way! Of course, Dan appreciated all the good will but I could tell by his voice that he knew deep down he really wouldn't be here next year and he was accepting that fact.

With very few exceptions, our metal detecting fraternity doesn't usually keep in touch throughout the year, so we have no idea what is currently happening in each of our lives. We wait to meet each other at the same spot, same time every year! We respect each other so much that we all wait to see who has finally arrived and has set up before we begin to go in the water to search. We line up around the swim area and stand there until each detectorist has his favorite shoreline position. When everyone is in place, a hand is waved by each and you can hear the phrases yelled across the water such as, "good luck", "save some for me", or "find my diamond ring" as we all begin wading in the water.

Call it strange but that unwritten rule of respect for each other is repeated every year. Once in the water, we all take a quick glance at each other and see who's finding jewelry or trash and who's still wading about with their head down listening for the ring tone of treasure. Funny how we all pass one another in the water within several feet and, sometimes, our machines that are on the same search frequency will interfere with each other, so we just smile and slowly wade further apart so as not to hinder anyone's experience. Every once in a while, someone will take a break, turn off their machine and wade over to see what's been found and hear the stories of how difficult or easy it was to retrieve targets. All good conversation and welcomed by all. Even the newbies quickly understand the pecking order and fit right in!

I explain all this because I want you to understand that when the next year DID roll by, Dan was not there and, as he predicted, he had passed away. I didn't really know Dan at all except from seeing him there year after year and talking at our vehicles as we put on our gear while waiting for others to arrive. But the thought of not seeing him again struck a place in my heart and brought my own mortality to the surface.

Later that year, someone mailed me a copy of his obituary and, as I read it, I felt I had known Dan as well as those included in the write up. I took a moment and wrote a personal note to Dan's wife telling her how much Dan had meant to all of us who had known him from metal detecting and how much we all enjoyed Dan's company, and that he'd be sorely missed! I wished her the best and told her she would in our prayers. I never did, or even expected to hear back from her, but I felt the urge to let her know that we had also lost someone that we had become friends with over the years. I hope that note gave her some comfort during her time of grief.

Now getting back to my original story, this particular time there happened to be nine of us detecting in the water and several detecting on the beach. Suddenly the park employee in question approached the water's edge and yelled out..."Need to see your permits!"

Here we all were, deep in our treasure hunt, and this guy wanted us to all come out of the water at that exact time to show him our permits? I didn't want to leave the water at that particular time so I politely yelled back from the water, "Hey, will you be working in this area for a while? We'll be out in a little bit and we can then meet at that time?"

I could see that he was extremely frustrated that we all didn't respond back to him quickly enough, so he then took his cigarette out of his mouth and yelled even louder, "Outta the water.....NOW!"

Of course, it made me mad that he would want to disrupt our enjoyment by exercising his limited authority as a park employee (not security, police or management) and make all nine of us shut down our gear and wade out of the water to furnish our permits. He could see we were all adults and seniors who were obviously aware of our responsibilities and not young teenagers trying to get away with something. Absolutely he had no respect or concern for us and was only interested exercising his own control and authority.

Grudgingly, we all waded out of the water and he inspected each permit. When he came to me I explained that my permit was in my car, over the visor, and I could show him later if he was going to be around. He wouldn't hear of it and demanded that we walk to the car that very moment so I could produce the permit right then and there! I was furious with his demand and as we walked together back to the vehicles, I told him I didn't care for his attitude and that what he was doing, although permitted, was not an ethical thing to do to a bunch of older guys. He could have handled the situation much better.

Not to mention the fact that I had taken time off from work and had traveled over 300 miles round trip to be here for this event and he was cutting into the short time that I had to metal detect.

He then told me that he was also a detectorist and I replied, "Then you of all people should have known better and should have shown us some respect! You know what a pain in the butt it is to wade in and out of water with full gear on!"

He continued to be obnoxious and copied down my name and address from my permit and told me that I wouldn't be allowed to water search there again. He would see to it that I was banned from entering the park.

I replied to him, "First, you don't have the authority and, if I ever find out that you attempted to do that, I'll take this issue all the way up to the State of New York!" Once he saw my permit, he reluctantly walked away, but not without muttering something under his breath. Not sure, but I'm sure it wasn't anything flattering!

When I finally got back home, I called the New York State Park Regional Director and explained what had taken place and that being at that park at that time each year was so much more than just metal detecting. Being banned from participating because of someone's obnoxious attitude was just not reasonable or acceptable.

The director listened to my entire story and told me that he had heard several other complaints regarding that particular park employee and that he would look into the situation. Later that summer the director called me directly and assured me that neither I or my brother Fred would be banned from searching in this park and we would be welcome there as in the past. He apologized for his employee's behavior.

When we returned the following year, we noticed that park employee was not around and probably had been reassigned to a different area of responsibility. Truly a "win-win" situation for all involved.

 Lesson here? **Tip #41:** *It's not WHAT you say, it's HOW you say it!*

Find New Places to Search

During the off months of winter, it's a good time to do some research and find new locations to search. There are many ways to do this and I'll explain a couple that you may not be aware of that have been very helpful to me.

Check local town maps. Google "old maps" and find the area that you would like to search. Check out the topographical maps, old maps, and aerial views. Check local history and see if there was any military activity in your area.

When you look at a topographical map, you'll see little black squares that are homesteads that were present when the map was produced. Many times those homes are no longer there and now it might be a field or maybe just woods at present day. You will also see roads that are no longer around, but remember, there was human activity back then and that would cause you to believe there must be treasure of some sort buried in the ground waiting for you to discover.

I haven't done this yet, but I plan on printing a "current road map" on a clear piece of plastic and then overlaying that on the same area of an older topographical map of the same area. Which would give me a clear view of how the territory has changed. I'm sure there would be homes that are no longer around or visible and those areas would need visiting. Remember, homes have people and people lose things. All kinds of things! It's your responsibility to go find those things and enjoy digging them up and adding them to your collection!

Find a Real Estate Friend

Real Estate agents have access to a tremendous amount of property information pertaining to the areas where they conduct most of their business. They can run a query on the homes in your area and they can tell you how old the homes are, where they're located, who owns them, and even the name and address. They can also give you a picture of the tax map and the property boundaries so you can see what the area looks like from above.

There's a plethora of information that a real estate agent can provide that is open to the public, but most people don't have the time to research it or know how to retrieve it. As an agent, I can take a section of town and print off every house's age in ascending or descending order, select the ones I'd like to visit, and then contact the owner by phone or mail and ask permission for access.

Most people think that nothing could possibly be found around a house that's in the city without much yard area. However, we don't know if the dirt around the house is the same dirt from when they initially dug the footing or if it was brought in from another location. You don't need a large amount of ground to metal detect and, chances are, you'll be the first one there! I've found a lot of nice items on small patches of dirt in and around older homes and businesses.

Don't rule out inner city areas where most people wouldn't even think of metal detecting. Visit with a friend and you might find out those areas can be very rewarding. But you'll need to use common sense and always ask permission regardless of where you decide to use your metal detector.

Curt & Carl and a Maine Beach

When you vacation at the same particular spot year after year, you begin to notice the same people year after year and, one day, you begin talking to them. Shortly thereafter, you might even become friends.

Curt and Carl are two of the nicest guys you would want to meet. They both metal detect at a particular Maine beach and we continually run into them every year while we're there on vacation. We have enjoyed so many laughs and have had so much fun together that my family and I look forward to seeing them every year!

Curt lives there locally and has the opportunity to search the shoreline almost every day of the year, including during winter. In fact, Curt tells me he has the best finds during the winter months. Go figure. He's a "hard searching" detectorist. He doesn't give up easily and has found some terrific items that he enjoys ribbing me about when he shows them to me. All in fun. We have a ton of laughter over it and we always try and "out find" each other every year. Curt usually wins. He's quick to remind me when it's time for me to go back home to NY. Which also happens to be when his daily discoveries start to slow down during our vacation week. Ha! I take that as a compliment.

I had to laugh when Curt told me one day that he knew of an area near the beach about 30 yards off shore by a huge rock that had a "cut". He said that cut probably held some gold. Well, it wasn't long before I searched that cut and recovered two nice gold wedding bands! You can imagine how long it took me to scoot over and show them to Curt. It had been a rough day in the ocean with high waves and large caps, but I fought against them and won, and I did thank Curt for the tip!

Curt has been extremely gracious, allowing me and my family to use some of his metal detecting equipment while we are there on vacation. It's always nice to try different machines and see how they perform. Yes, it's been a pleasure to know Curt and we all look forward to seeing him again this summer!

Carl is a lot like my own family who travel from out of state and vacation at the same spot every year. We've been able to connect each year and enjoy each other's company. Again, like Curt, Carl is quite a guy and we all look forward to seeing him again this summer. We always exchange metal detecting stories and share common interests in many other things. Metal detecting has brought us many nice friends and acquaintances over the years!

Dave and the Gold Wedding Band

I had a few days off from work so I planned on hitting one of my favorite public swim areas early one Monday morning. I arrived very early as usual and the day was perfect. A nice sun rise, warm weather and the water was calm as can be.

As I entered the water I noticed another detectorist already in the water farther down the shoreline. Seeing him didn't discourage me at all, since I've mentioned all along that no one detectorist can find it all and there's plenty of treasure to go around. I was simply surprised to see someone else shallow water searching this early on a weekday morning, at this particular swim area.

I searched my way toward the other detectorist and noticed that, along the way, my signals were few and far between. Usually by now, I would have several clad coins and possibly some jewelry in my pouch, however, this was not the case this particular morning. When I got close enough to recognize who the other detectorist was, I realized it was a fellow detectorist Dave who is a very dedicated treasure hunter himself. It's always a pleasure to share stories with Dave.

When we finally met, we both stopped searching to say hello. I told Dave that I thought it was unusual that I hadn't had many signals thus far. He said he was experiencing the same results. He mentioned that a new person had just gotten hooked on shallow water searching and that he was in the water every single day like clockwork. He would spend hours and hours searching the area. In fact, Dave said he thought the guy actually had fish gills since he was in the water so much!

We laughed about a lot of things and talked about the future possibility of getting together for an Island trip someday. It's always nice to have a dream. We shook hands, told each other good luck, fired up our detectors and parted ways.

I got about twenty yards away from Dave when I hit a strong signal. Finally! It had been quite a while since I had had a signal of any kind, including trash, so I was quite excited. As I located the target and raised my scoop up from the water, I looked inside the scoop and saw the glimmer of gold reflecting the early morning sunrise. What a sight to see! Sweeeeet!

There, in the bottom of my water scoop was a beautiful, older style, 24K gold wedding band! You can imagine my excitement. Here I was getting a little concerned myself about not finding very much that morning, as well as hearing about a new detectorist named Neil who was spending most of his time searching in the same area for hours upon hours every day; it seemed appropriate that I would NOT be hearing many signals. I had to keep reminding myself that regardless of how many people are shallow water metal detecting, they still can't find it all!

Of course, that's much easier to do when you're thinking about it while you're sitting in your recliner at home, but when you're out here in the water wading about and there's a long lull between signals, a lot different thoughts go through your mind. Although I've said many times before, never, never give up, at this point, I needed to listen to my own advice.

I called out to Dave and waved to him to come back over and see what I had just found. Once he took a look at the gold ring I had found, he was simply amazed. Like me, he was reassured that no one can find ALL the treasure and there is plenty to go around.

Regardless of finding that beautiful gold ring or not, it would have been an enjoyable day. Just being outside searching in the calm lake water on such a great day and taking in the sights was a pleasure enough. Running into my friend Dave made it that much more special. Never give up!

My Brother Bill & His Schoolhouse

My older brother Bill and I vacationed together with our families in southern California, about 40 years ago. He absolutely fell in love with the area so much that he returned shortly thereafter with his entire family to settle down.

He bought an old schoolhouse building from the 1800's with a bell tower on the top that had been sitting vacant for many years. He and his family remodeled the interior, according to that era, and his daughter began using the school house as a wedding venue. She started doing so much business, that they had to expand, which meant that they would need to enlarge the parking lot, first by expanding the current dirt area and then by paving over it.

Bill is aware of my passion for metal detecting and he had asked me if I wanted to search the area before he had it completely paved. Of course, I said sure and I that I would combine that with a trip to visit him and his family at the same time.

My wife and I arrived at Bill's home in Southern CA about two weeks later. It wasn't long before Bill and I were walking the old school house property together, me, with my metal detector and Bill walking along side of me. Bill has no real interest in detecting and I can understand that, but still, he's very supportive. He watched as I located and dug up several Indian head pennies, a few wheat pennies, and a couple of newer memorial pennies.

After we had been searching for about two hours I began to see that Bill was being as supportive as he could be. However, there was a limit to his patience, especially doing an activity he wasn't actually that interested in. I suggested that we head back to our car and we continued to search as we walked back, Bill asked me, "Why don't you turn the machine off as we walk back to the car?" I replied, "Hey, you never know. Can't take a chance on missing anything. Once this area's paved, it's gone forever!"

We got within about ten feet of our car and we were about two feet from the edge of the main road when I got a nice signal. Bill watched as I dug up a beautiful 1864 Seated Liberty quarter! Such a shiny piece of solid silver laying only three inches under the hard dirt. Probably been sitting there for over a hundred years! A welcomed sight indeed and such a nice way to finish an already enjoyable morning! Let me remind you, at the risk of sounding redundant, _never_ turn your machine off and give up on a search until you actually reach your end destination. I've said it many times before. It could be the very last key on the keyring that opens the lock.

Cleaning Your Treasure

Whatever you do, be sure not to clean your coins to the point of wearing off the dates and identification. Coins are worth much more in their natural state as found. I know they look better all bright and shiny but don't fall prey to the thought that a pretty, shiny coin is worth more than a dull one. Collectors like to see coins in the most original condition they were found in.

I usually take a soft toothbrush and use liquid dish soap to lightly wash off the surface dirt and, once identifiable, I put the rare dated ones in a plastic bag with a little bit of olive oil. The olive oil keeps the coins moist and easier to lightly clean second time around.

In the case of regular clad coins, I put them in a rock tumbler along with a handful of stones from a fish aquarium, a little water, and baking soda. Let them tumble overnight. You'd be amazed at how clean a rock tumbler makes the coins.

Tip # 42: *Be sure to keep the same denominations of coins together when tumbling. Example, all quarters together, or all dimes, etc. Do not mix them as they will turn color during the tumbling process.*

I live in a part of the country that freezes over each winter for at least four months, and that's a long time for me to go without swinging a coil and finding treasure! Absolutely sheer torture! So I take advantage of my down time to clean my treasure and research new detecting locations using Google and old maps.

If you are lucky to live in an area that is warm most of the year then you are extremely fortunate. Take advantage of the geographical area in which you live and find the best places to detect!

Mustard-Relish-Beach Prank

Metal detectorists can be a great source of fun for those who are not participating in the sport and for those who have no idea how dedicated and serious a detectorist can be while searching for treasure! This is why I said earlier that if you plan on metal detecting, better put on a tough outer skin to ward off jokesters and pranksters who get a kick out of funning with and kidding around with a detectorist.

Case in point: Whenever I have a hot dog or "Coney", it's very important to me to have mustard and pickle relish on my dogs! Not sure why, but without those two ingredients, the dogs just don't taste good and, quite frankly, they're not even worth eating. Hey, call it strange, call it odd, but in the end, a hot dog without those condiments might as well be a piece of leather in a bun to me!

Every year, several Black Belts from my Karate school overnight together in Sandwich Maine on our way to Martha's Vineyard for a long weekend. While at the Cape, I always take advantage of shallow water searching. Well, a few of my fellow Black Belts heard me talk about my obsession with mustard and relish on my hot dogs and they decided to pull a fast one on me.

That night, a Shodan (first degree Black Belt) asked me if she could go with me on my next land search while at the Cape. I thought that was strange as she had never expressed an interest in my metal detecting, but this time she seemed overly anxious to come along with me, so I obliged her and just about 8:30 PM we set out together from our camp and worked our way through the woods down toward the beach area. She continually asked me a bunch of questions and seemed extremely interested in every located target along the way. Odd, I thought, since she had never seemed that interested before, but it was nice that someone really enjoyed the sport as much as myself and was trying to learn all about it.

As we worked our way through the woods heading toward the beach area, she helped by holding the flashlight as I dug each target. We continued to find pennies and trash along the way until we finally made it to the beach.

Once we reached the beach she kept suggesting we head in a particular direction, but my instincts sent me a different way until, finally, it was too late to continue, so we headed back to the cabin for the night with the suggestion that we return to the beach the next morning.

When we arrived at the cabin, we were all discussing the beach barbecue earlier and how much better the hot dogs *would* have tasted had they had some mustard and/or relish on them. We all laughed and I continued to bust on them as to how anyone could forget such important condiments for the hot dogs when planning a barbecue! All in fun, all good.

The next morning, I headed back to the beach and sure enough, there was my fellow Black Belt right beside me! Wow, I thought to myself....she really must like metal detecting to be up this early and accompanying me to the beach. Once again, as we reached the beach she suggested we try a different area and I agreed. Not aware that she was steering me toward a particular area, we continued finding clad coins and other nondescript items until I reached an area with an exceptionally strong signal.

She seemed happy as she watched me dig down about a foot to retrieve the target. As I dug deeper, she continued to smile and when I reached the target, she exploded with laughter! It was a brand new jar of pickle relish that the others had buried in the hopes that I would have found it before we barbecued the ho dogs the night before!

That event created laughter for all of us for the entire trip and still brings a smile to my face whenever I remember that moment!

Yes, metal detecting is an activity that few understand yet many are curious about. Even fewer would ever take the time to research the sport or decide to get involved. It's not easy and, when you think about it, finding a dime after an intense search in all kinds of weather, *REALLY?* One dime? One tenth of a dollar would actually excite someone? If the value of the treasure is your objective then I would suggest that you consider selecting a different activity. As I always mention to the many curious bystanders when they ask me what am I looking for...... I smile and reply, "Stay in school and get a good education and you won't have to do this for a living!" You should see all the smiles!

My wife Maria, Vicki and me digging up the famous "pickle relish" beach treasure!

Shodan Vicki and I recover the jar of pickle relish! Plenty of laughs to go around on this prank!

Random Shots

Here's my wife and me on Daytona Beach. Had a fun day and a much needed break from the cold weather up north! Still found a bunch of clad coins even in the off season.

One week's jewelry find on a Maine beach!

Hitting the rocky area. Most detectorists ignore the "hard to walk" areas. I found one of my oldest rings in these rocks! It's very difficult to walk on these rocks, let alone try and dig with your scoop. You'll be using your hand digging tool more often than not in this kind of situation. Lots of rock turning but, trust me, the treasure is within! Most detectorists don't even take the time and effort to conquer these mini mountains.

Another Daytona Beach day! Notice the "cut" area. That's where the water has collected and that's usually where jewelry ends up at the end of the day. Don't forget to check these areas out before you leave the beach!

Don't be overwhelmed with the vast area in front of you. It's very easy to think that it's too big to search, but trust me, there's treasure there just waiting to be found by you. Will it take a while? Absolutely, but enjoy your time while searching by noticing all the things around you!

Worst case scenario? You find a couple of clad coins but you felt the wind and sun and listened to the surf as you walked along the beach doing something for yourself that you really enjoy. What better way to spend some much needed relaxing time!

And remember.....if it was easy, then everyone would be doing it! Good luck!

Taking a break on a California beach. A terrific day!
Notice the probe attached to my metal detector. It is so
helpful in locating targets quickly. Be sure to get
yourself one. They can mount on the shaft or be
carried separately. I happen to have both for different
searches.

Showing my brother-in-law how to use my metal detector. Like any sport, it always appears easier to do than it actually is and some quick instructions go a long way!

A nice gold & diamond ring just as I dug it from the hard pan! Sweeeeeeet!!!!! What a rush when you find one of these!

Another view once I cleared the sand out from the center!

I found this ring about 30 yards from the previous one, the same day and about 20 minutes later! Amazing and hard to believe since this particular area gets searched every single day (and night)! Hey, they still can't find it all!

A different beach area in Maine. Hard to believe that there is coin and jewelry just below the surface of what you're looking at now. So much area to search and with so little time.

California beach searching. Ended up with about three dollars in about one hour. Didn't see one detectorist out there all day. Just felt nice being there! Priceless.

Metal detecting with my good friend Jimmy as we do every year! He had a ball just hanging with me as we searched along the shoreline. I dug up a silver spoon from the 1800's and gave it to him. He was so excited and we bonded a lot together that sunny afternoon. As I've said, it's so much more than just metal detecting!

Found myself on a quick trip to the Cape without my water scoop so I improvised and got heckled by everyone there that night, but guess what? I found some nice coin and one ring with that contraption! (A broom handle duct taped onto my hand scoop).

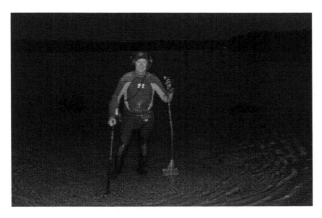

I absolutely love summer night water searching! Here I am coming out of the water from a successful night search. No rings but lots of coin! A beautiful Cape Cod summer night. Peaceful and serene! People must wonder, what in the world is that guy doing in the water at night? If they only knew.

My brother-in-law Richard with his son Zac. They were using
my first detector and found several nice coins that day.
More importantly, they were spending time together which
proves once more that it's so much more than just metal
detecting!

Low tide on a Maine beach with a beautiful sunrise at 4:00 in the morning. These are some of the wonderful sites a metal detectorist experiences while on a search.

Equipment used about $1200, value of the finds that day about $200, viewing a Maine sunrise.....absolutely priceless!!!!

A freshly groomed beach in Maine just waiting for someone like me, and a million others like me, to come along and discover some coins or a lost piece of jewelry.

This doesn't look too exciting to a beachgoer, but to a detectorist it's a great spot to find a bunch of stuff! Those rocks capture more things and keep them from heading out to sea. Yes, that includes trash, but I always take it back to shore and dispose of it properly!

My brother-in-law Richard and his son Zac digging up what later turned out to be a beautiful silver ring caught in the deep mud!

A quick view of my treasure chest "Box of Tears". It
has grown quite a bit since this picture was taken, but you
can understand why I have so much interest in this
activity! Other photos in this book show several of the
items I have found over the years. To say it's been
interesting would be an understatement. So many great
and memorable experiences along the way and hopefully,
so many more to come!

My nephew Zac in Daytona Florida and with his special Birthday cake that had a metal detector decoration. Tell me he's not hooked on metal detecting!

An example of a tax map property outline.

My Real Estate profile picture.

My wife Maria is a fourth degree Black Belt (Sensei) and I am a third degree Black Belt in traditional Japanese Karate. My martial arts training has enabled me to metal detect in difficult locations at all hours of the day and still have enough strength to make it back to my vehicle! Staying healthy has been my mission in life and, as a result, I enjoy outdoor activities to the fullest. You can too!

Get yourself involved in some type of exercise program, even it's only going for daily walks. It's all beneficial for you and has long lasting rewards.

My work bench area where all of my finds eventually end up.

My son Phil Jr. and my grandkids, (left to right) Carter, Aiden and Spencer. Enjoying our annual Father's Day camping trip where we spend precious time together making memories that last a lifetime. Priceless.

A packed beach in Maine on summer afternoon! I call everyone depositors. They leave behind all kinds of stuff behind for me to come along and discover!

A Maine beach at low tide. Plenty of hard pan area to search!

Our daughter, Alexandria (center) who is a producer for ABC News, GMA in NYC. She let us have our picture taken while sitting at the anchors' desk! Quite an experience for us!

I was driving by this sidewalk that was under construction and asked permission to detect it. Received permission and found a nice musket ball. I gave it to the guy in charge for allowing me to search the area. He was extremely happy!

Sorry for the blurred picture. After about two hours of searching I found these items at an old farmhouse. The owner reluctantly gave me permission and told me I wouldn't find anything because other detectorists had been there before me. As I've said a million times......they can't find everything! Here's proof. That's a gold ring, silver pocket compact, and several wheat and Indian head pennies. Not bad for a place that didn't have anything!

My friend and real estate broker, Janet, on a property that she got us permission to search. A revolutionary military camping area that yielded some very interesting items in the short hour we were there. The scenery was absolutely breathtaking. We'll be back when we have more time. Meanwhile, visions of what can possibly be there continue to float around in my head. Janet now says she needs her own detector.

This is how it looked when I found this State of Alabama ring on the way up from the Cape Cod beach area on a logging trail. It was about eight inches deep in the soil. It always pays to detect all the way back to the vehicle. Sometimes it's the last key on the keyring that opens the lock. Here's proof.

My wonderful wife Maria. She has no interest in metal detecting but supports me 100% just the same.

I took this picture as I was walking to the lighthouse near a beach in Maine. I couldn't resist what this picture was saying.....come sit and relax and enjoy what God has given you this day. Sunlight, warmth, beautiful ocean and the health to enjoy it all. A perfect case of a picture that is worth a thousand, no, make that a million words!

found an old jackknife, three memorial pennies, one
ndian head penny and a quarter next to this walkway. Not
;ure how coins and things end up in tiny areas like this
)ut don't disregard small areas for metal detecting.
;ometimes they hold treasures you can't imagine.

I found a nice silver dime and several wheat pennies in the front yard of this 1850 Greek revival home that I had just listed for sale. The owner walked alongside me as we found each target. He was amazed at the items that were laying in his yard all those years. He has invited me back to search the rest of the property. I'll definitely give him a call!

hope you found this book both interesting and informative. he information contained here is as accurate as possible. I so wanted to share with you some of my personal xperiences with you that were relevant to metal detecting. I ave you 42 Tips along the way and kept them within the opics being discussed at that time. Hopefully, this way, the ps will be more meaningful to you and easier to remember.

hould you decide to take up this unusual hobby or if you are urrently directly involved with it, you'll soon find that you are ither hooked completely or just not interested at all. Those of s that are hooked, are just that....hooked!

have met a lot of people who also metal detect and, I have to ay, I've never come across an unfriendly one yet. They always eem eager to engage in conversation and offer whatever help hey can. As I mentioned earlier on, metal detecting means so nuch more to me than simply walking around with a metal haft that has a coil on the bottom. This hobby has helped me ond with friends and family and has given me an opportunity o literally touch history.

Vhen I dig up an old coin or ring, I think of the person it elonged to originally. I wonder what the circumstances were urrounding the purchase and the loss of the item. What type of person owned it? Was it Karma that caused them to lose it or ust simply bad luck? Regardless of how and why it was lost, he fact remains that it laid right there in that spot from the day t hit the ground until I came along and discovered it! I wish ou the best of luck in your new sport and, for those who are urrently involved, I hope I've shared some useful information with you and that you at least take away something memorable rom one of the 42 tips I have listed along the way.

This is some of the treasure that I have discovered over the years. Remember, that each item (and there are literally thousands here) was individually located as a target and then recovered either from the land or from under the water.

The containers to the right hold thousands of coins and odd objects yet to be cleaned. The boxes on the left hold coins that have already been cleaned and sorted.

I thought you'd like to see what you can expect to find while metal detecting in your area. To me, every item is a treasure of some sort and exciting to find regardless of its monetary value. Hopefully, you'll feel the same way and enjoy your new activity to the fullest!

This is a collage that my wife put together of my collection and I liked it so much I thought I would include it in this book!

It's never too early to learn the art of metal detecting. Here I am showing my daughter Alex and nephew Mark some tips on using a metal detector. We found several clad coins on this Florida beach.

My nephew Zac is learning the art of shallow water searching by following me in the water. Most of my treasures have been found at this depth!

In Closing

don't claim to know everything there is to know about metal detecting, but I have enjoyed what I have learned and I continue to learn something new every time I venture out to search an area. It has now been almost 15 years since I started this as a hobby and it is still as exciting for me as it was the first day I began!

Metal detectorists are a special breed of people. They're part archeologist, detective, coin collector, treasure hunter and just curious people with a desire to explore the unknown and feel the rush of a discovery. Then they enjoy sharing their adventures with others.

As I get older in life and I have experienced so many different things along the way and surprises are not as frequent as they were in my youth. However, metal detecting continues to give me the thrill of the hunt. Rewards come in many different forms and searching for the unknown provides that excitement. As I write this book, my brother Fred is still quite ill and I hope that he is well enough once again to read and enjoy what I have written. I have learned a lot from him and his own metal detecting experiences and I've passed that same information along for those who are interested.

Many thanks to my beautiful and understanding wife Maria, (and daughter Alex), who put up with my last minute trips to the water's edge before a sunset, or to an old farm that I had just heard about and received permission to search. Or the time my wife sat patiently in the car and waited as I put my wet suit on and waded out into the crashing water with my brand new metal detector that I had just purchased. I couldn't wait another day to try it out! The list of thanks and appreciation could go on for pages, but more importantly is the fact that there is so much more to metal detecting than just finding stuff. I hope you experience some of the same things I have!

Good luck and God Bless!

Thanks Fred

xox

Made in the USA
Middletown, DE
03 October 2020

21048125R00080